The Journey Along the Narrow Way

(Jesus Led Me All the Way)

James Perry

The Journey Along the Narrow Way

Library of Congress Control Number: 2018936830

ISBN 9780998560670

DEDICATION

To dedicate a book to someone is not always an easy task. In my life, there have been several people and churches that have been a positive influence. The closeness in relationship with each has grown deeper as the years have passed.

However, there is one person with whom I have had a personal relationship all of my earthly life – my sister – Ruth Perry Kuttruf. Ruth is older than I and has always had a propensity to look after her "baby" brother. We were born during the years of the Great Depression and life was not very easy. There were limited resources and to indicate times were hard would be an understatement.

Amid it all, with difficulties and challenges, Ruth has always been an example and encouragement to me. She could've easily become bitter with life but that was never a part of her personal DNA. Her tender and caring heart has always been obvious. We continue to spend time visiting together on the telephone and she remains the very positive, caring and encouraging person.

Early on, she was always church-oriented and participated in various capacities in church ministry. She played in a church trumpet trio and was an active participant in outdoor evangelism ministry in Columbus Circle, NYC. It meant that she would often travel on the Subway System to return home alone. She did so with confidence in the Lord that He would watch over and protect her – and He always did and has! Her example has been contagious and I do not have enough words to share how important she continues to be in my life and how very much I appreciate her kind and caring words.

It is my joy and privilege to dedicate this book to my sister and friend – Ruth Perry Kuttruf.

Foreword

It was one of the greatest privileges of my life to study under the late Evangelical Christian leader, Chuck Colson. He taught that the root of today's cultural decay is a direct result of America's abandonment of the Judeo/Christian Worldview. In many ways, Pastor James Perry picks up Colson's Biblical Worldview torch and runs with it.

The Journey Along The Narrow Way establishes that there is really such a thing as TRUTH. TRUTH is a concept today's Progressives reject with zeal. Biblical Truth is the backbone of the Biblical Worldview which America has cast aside to favor a Progressive Worldview, arrogantly rejecting and often condemning the guidance of the One True God. James Perry's book is loaded with examples of today's chaos, which is a direct result of our culture proudly embracing LGBT rights, abortion, gay marriage, and gender neutrality, to name a few. Our author is quite correct in stating that the way back to a country with values like those we were raised with is indeed "narrow."

Building on TRUTH, James Perry's readers are asked to reflect upon Christ and how he lived when he became Man and walked the earth. The foundation of the book is as crystal clear as Hillsong, when they sing: It's All about You Jesus. Perry puts it this way: We need to spend quality time with God as we ponder Him and His Greatness. Each of the chapters leave the reader with a point to ponder which stays with you long after the book is set aside for the day.

Perry reflects on those living on the margins of our society. Like Colson, he puts emphasis on prison ministry and others suffering alone, such as widows, orphans and the sick. The book is often tender, as accounts of loved ones and folks that have touched a pastor's heart over a long and fruitful career are recounted. Pastor Perry brings the Bible alive in these stories.

The Journey Along The Narrow Way glorifies our Living God.

Sue Ann Thielke
Colson Fellow

INTRODUCTION

Jesus Christ made a distinction between The Narrow Pathway and the Broad Way. In the Sermon on the Mount, Matthew 7:13-14 (BSB – Berean Study Bible), Jesus said: "Enter through the narrow gate. For wide is the gate and broad is the way that leads to destruction, and many enter through it. But small is the gate and narrow the way that leads to life, and only a few find it." When Jesus indicated that only a few find the narrow way, He is indicating that individual discipline and commitment are vital to one both finding the narrow way and continuing on it. Admittedly, there will be distractions that occur where choices must be made. At such a moment, do I continue along this narrow way even though it is difficult to do so, or do I allow myself to determine an alternative that is less rigid?

This book will reference some of the distractions and unexpected moments where a decision must be made. Will my choice keep me on the narrow way, or will a lesser general consensus become an alternative choice? At least two Scripture references should be included and factored in whenever alternatives occur. The first is Hebrews 12:1-2 that reminds us that a spiritual commitment includes seeing the bigger picture and determining to patiently endure because one's eyes will be fixed upon Jesus Christ who endured and walked this same narrow way.

A second Biblical instruction is the testimony of the Apostle Paul in Philippians 3:13-14. Once again, the guidance is to forget the past and to focus on the future. It will require a personal discipline and genuine effort to be totally focused on Jesus Christ as one presses on to what is ahead.

Some of you regularly read the Blogs that I post. It was suggested to me that I consider expanding some of them and publish them in book form. I consider it a privilege to do so and to share these perspectives and reality moments with you.

May they refresh your soul and spirit. May they bless and enrich your life. To God be all the Glory!

James Perry

Table of Contents

1. Spiritual Miscues

Perspective and Reality Moment

Taking a serious God condescendingly, flippantly or matter-of-factly is becoming too common-place in a culture that is adrift from its spiritual moorings and values. One can hear expressions, usually profane, that make use of the name "Jesus Christ" and "My God" – but they are empty, meaningless and valueless words. In religious settings, one can also hear the name of God and Jesus Christ but too often it is lofty rhetoric. Jesus indicated as much when He stated, Matthew 15:7-9, "You hypocrites! Isaiah prophesied correctly about you: These people honor Me with their lips, but their hearts are far from Me. They worship Me in vain; they teach as doctrine the precepts of men."

The words of Jesus are penetrating. How often do we approach Him casually rather than purposefully; matter-of-factly rather than earnestly; ritualistically rather than with an obedient faith. We call out to "God" when confronting an emergency or uncertainty. Are we doing so with a sense of desperation more than dependence? Is Psalm 84:1-2 our earnest desire and reality: "How lovely is your dwelling place, Lord Almighty! My soul yearns, even faints, for the courts of the Lord; my heart and my flesh cry out for the Living God"?

In an A.W. Tozer Devotional, the following verses are quoted: "The Lord said to Joshua: Stand up! What are you doing down on your face? Israel has sinned; they have violated my covenant...That is why the Israelites cannot stand against their enemies...because they have been made liable to destruction. I will not be with you anymore unless you destroy whatever among you is devoted to destruction" (Joshua 7:10-12). In desperate times, people more steeped in traditions or superstitions will pray to anything or anyone as they hope for relief or deliverance from a situation that is marginal or with which one is incapable of coping. This is a reason why so many nationals world-wide continue to pray to gods of their own making and choosing – idols, martyrs, saints (so-designated). They hope that their repetitious recitations, incantations, with obeisance (deferential respect) will somehow bring about a desired result. It is not dissimilar to a good luck orientation and practice – four leaf clovers, rabbit's feet, beads, medals and/or medallions.

What does Jesus Christ indicate as the correct way to pray for and seek spiritual benefit? John 14:13-14, "I will do whatever you ask in My name, so that the Father may be glorified in the Son. If you ask Me anything in My name, I will do it." Additional guidance in this regard is Romans 8:26-27, "The Spirit helps us in our weakness. For we do not know how we ought to pray, but the Spirit Himself intercedes for us with groans too deep for words. And He who searches our hearts knows the mind of the Spirit, because the Spirit intercedes for the saints according to the will of God."

To whom or what do you pray? The manner in which you pray, is it tantamount to a spiritual miscue or is it consistent with Biblical instruction and directive? First Timothy 2:5-6 instructs: "There is one God and one mediator between God and men, the man Christ Jesus, who gave Himself as a ransom for all." Why not pray to and through Him alone? He declared (John 14:6), "I am the way, the truth and the life." Since Jesus Christ alone is the only way, we should come confidently to Him with our needs, burdens, requests. Along with that confidence, we should also come with a grateful heart and be thankful to Him. Jesus never promised that the journey along the narrow way would be easy. He did promise to be with you all along that path. A wise Bible teacher reminded his students: "The secret of guidance is the guide" (Proverbs 3:5-6). Prayerfully – consider these things with me.

1. Spiritual Miscues

To Remember:

If the Lord said His grace is sufficient,
then believe that His grace is sufficient for you!

2. Disgustingly Human

Perspective and Reality Moment

A Seminary professor once shared in a class on practical ministry that one of the things a young minister will discover early on is that people are disgustingly human. Some of them can and will be roadblocks that limit church ministry effectiveness. A book was published several years ago by Dr. Steve Brown where he referred to some in a church leadership role as "well-intentioned dragons."

The original title for this chapter was Bête Noire which is defined as: "a person or thing especially disliked or dreaded." The Thesaurus adds the following: "adversary; anathema; bane; enemy; competitor; opponent; rival." It is inevitable in one's life – both physical and spiritual – that a Bête Noire situation will arise. The question is not IF it will occur but WHEN it occurs – how will one respond or react to it? It can occur in various forms and manner. There are two possible ways to deal with this situation: First, retaliate in kind or Second, humbly accept it as falling within God's plan for one's life. This would be similar to Joseph when he had the power to retaliate against his brothers, but instead concluded (Genesis 50:20) "As for you, you meant evil against me, but God meant it for good, to bring it about that many people should be kept alive, as they are today."

It is difficult to step back and let a colleague or an arrogant fellow-believer dominate, gaining recognition and winning a battle without his/her thought about losing the war. It can too easily become rabble rousing rather constructive thoughts or input. At such times and in such situations, one must manifest the quality of Jesus Christ that is indicated and recommended to be embraced in a practical way. Philippians 2:5-7 shares,

"You must have the same attitude that Christ Jesus had. Though he was God, he did not think of equality with God as something to cling to. Instead, he gave up his divine privileges; he took the humble position of a slave..." Will this be easy to do? No! Are we willing to assume the role of a slave/servant and be like Jesus? Unless this is done, the enemy of one's soul will have us ensnared, ineffective and unproductive (Second Peter 1:5-9).

In John 13:12-17, at the Passover Meal, Jesus first washes his disciples' feet. He then asks them:

> "Do you know what I have done for you? You call Me Teacher and Lord, and rightly so, because I am. So, if I, your Lord and Teacher, have washed your feet, you also should wash one another's feet. I have set you an example so that you should do as I have done for you. Truly, truly, I tell you, no servant is greater than his master, nor is a messenger greater than the one who sent him. If you know these things, you will be blessed if you do them."

There is no room for the display of bête noire here.

An additional illustration is contained in Matthew 5:3-12, The Beatitudes. Four highlights are: "Blessed are the poor in spirit... Blessed are the meek... Blessed are the peacemakers...Blessed are those who are persecuted because of righteousness, for theirs is the kingdom of heaven. Blessed are you when people insult you, persecute you, and falsely say all kinds of evil against you because of Me. Rejoice and celebrate, because great is your reward in heaven; for in the same way they persecuted the prophets before you."

Nowhere in Scripture is the biblical Christian encouraged to embrace a "Bête Noire" toward anyone or any circumstance. The guideline for response and reaction is Ephesians 4:32, "Be kind and tender-hearted to one another, forgiving each other just as in Christ God forgave you." These are character traits for the one whose journey is on the narrow way. Prayerfully – consider these things with me.

To Remember:

To love one's enemies is not an option
but it is a requirement declared by Jesus Christ.

3. Defining Moments

Perspective and Reality Moment

In a competitive world, how one is defined is important. Another factor pertains to who does the defining. In the area of politics, the more effective campaigns have been successful at defining any or all of their opponents. It is the art of painting a portrait of an individual. This tactic by an incumbent is to have the opponent spend his time and resources on arguing and defending against a negative. That is the plan and ploy as one candidate's staff (usually the incumbent), rightly or wrongly, frames the discussion by forcing the adversary to discuss what they wish to have discussed rather than discussing issues, current policies and/or failures of the incumbent. In other instances, profiling of a person or ethnic group occurs based solely on the language one uses or a suspicion about behavioral possibilities. Profiling is defined as: "using specific characteristics, as race or age, to make generalizations about a person, as whether he or she may be engaged in illegal activity."

It can occur in the Public-School system when a teacher or administrator becomes frustrated with a difficult student and enters into defining that student as incorrigible or one who will never amount to anything. If one teacher gives a student a D for his or her conduct (general deportment), each seceding teacher observes that label or profile and will probably give a similar opinion about the student's behavior regardless of whether or not it is accurate, fair or correct.

A person is often defined by others. If it occurs when a child is young, it leaves him/her with a sense of 'what's the use of trying' and he/she begin to live up to the image that has been created, as well as the expectation that has become established. Is it fair? No! Should it be allowed? No! Can the student overcome the psychological scar and be more than what others have defined him or her to be? Yes!

An example of this is the late Dr. Howard Hendricks, long-time Professor at Dallas Theological Seminary. In a biographical statement, he said:

> I was born into a broken home. My parents separated when I came along. I split the family. Reared by his father's mother, Dr. Hendricks said that in elementary school he was a troublemaker, a hell-raiser. Probably just acting out a lot of insecurities, he said looking back on his Philadelphia childhood. His fifth-grade teacher had predicted that five boys in class would end up in prison. He was supposed to be one of them. The teacher was right about three of them, Dr. Hendricks said. That teacher, Miss Simon, once tied him to his seat with a rope and taped his mouth shut. When he introduced himself to his sixth-grade teacher, Miss Noe, she told him something that would change his life forever. She said, 'I've heard a lot about you, but I don't believe a word of it,' he recalls. She made him realize for the first time in his life that someone cared, he says. People are always looking for someone to say, 'Hey, I believe in you.'

An interesting example of one who has been defined by the media occurred with Tim Tebow when he was associated with the New York Jets football team. When a false news report was circulated, in his attempt to defend himself, Tebow stated: "I think the only thing that's been disappointing these last few days and frustrating is people saying: 'Oh, you quit on your team, or you're not a good teammate.' For people who do not know the situation, and then start to bash your character and say you're a phony or you're a fake or you're a hypocrite,

I think that's what's disappointing... You work your whole life to build a reputation...Then people try to tear you down when they don't understand even what happened."

In a narrower sense, there is a profile for one who claims to be a Christian. There are character traits and expected behavior. At the outset of His ministry, Jesus Christ gave one of the characteristics in John 13:34-35 (NIV): "A new commandment I give you, that you love one another, as I have loved you. By this all will know that you are My disciples, if you have love for one another." This characteristic of love and a place for one to begin is stated in I Corinthians 13:4-8 (NLT), "Love is patient and kind. Love is not jealous or boastful or proud or rude. Love does not demand its own way. Love is not irritable, and it keeps no record of when it has been wronged. It is never glad about injustice but rejoices whenever the truth wins out. Love never gives up, never loses faith, is always hopeful, and endures through every circumstance. Love will last forever..."

Does this define who you are and what you consistently practice and display? When others are in your presence, do they have a sense that this is who you are or just an image you try to maintain and project when you are among "Christians" who expect you to behave in a certain way? Jesus meant what He said! Do you desire His requisite to be perfected in you? It is good to remember that what you are always speaks louder than what you say. Prayerfully – consider these things with me.

To Remember:

We are to be champions for the truth – not just in word but also by our actions.

4. Forgetting and Dementia

Perspective and Reality Moment

It's a given that we're all forgetful at times, regardless of our age and mental health. However, as we age, our risk of dementia increases, and by the age of 85 almost 35-percent in this age group will be afflicted with this degenerative disorder that causes gradually and worsening memory loss and mental skills. Some of the common symptoms of Dementia are: First, Memory Loss. It is an inability to recall short term memory (or recent events). A study from Rutgers University estimates that roughly 50-percent of all Americans over 85-years of age suffer with Alzheimer's Disease and that more than half of all dementia cases are misdiagnosed. Second, Behavioral Changes. Personality changes that may include the opposite manners or personality traits or just being inappropriate in public can signify the onset of dementia. Third, Cognitive Decline. This could be as simple as an inability to reason or a more drastic decline in cognitive functions – thinking, learning, reading and retaining information, problem solving, language and speech.

Within the body of Christ, the biblical Church, how should we respond to those who may be in some stage of dementia? Does the church know how to relate to one who struggles with dementia or who is closing in on Alzheimer's? A couple of guidelines that can be considered, learned and implemented are: First, Acceptance. Romans 15:7, "Accept one another just as Christ accepted you." Second, show kindness and understanding: Ephesians 4:32, "Be kind and compassionate to one another." Third, encouragement. Hebrews 10:25, "Encouraging one another." Fourth, prayer. James 5:13, "Is anyone among you in trouble? Let them pray!" Since so many are sketchy about mental health and those who are affected in some way with mental health issues, a tendency is to marginalize that struggling soul. That often means non-acceptance or avoidance. If a person has forgotten who you are, just smile and say – "I am Jane" or "I am Joe", etc. Special effort should be made to include the person who is mentally declining. It will require an increased measure of patience and encouragement by everyone.

A secular example of this care and assistance was seen in the life of Glen Campbell who was diagnosed with Alzheimer's in 2011. In 2014, a very compelling documentary about his journey and effort to cope, "I'll Be Me", was released. Part of the film shows him on a farewell concert tour as his condition worsened. One thing that stands out in the documentary is the acceptance and kind understanding of his family, staff, musicians and audiences.

After previewing the above comments, a friend wrote: "Thanks for your thoughts on forgetting/dementia. It was an encouragement to me as I try to care for my mother, especially in keeping her involved with the church family. She loves to attend all the services and she seems to feel comfortable there. I don't know how much of the preaching she comprehends, but I constantly pray that it causes some awareness of her relationship with the Lord. Most members of the church practice the guidelines you included, although a few Sunday morning attendees simply ask me about her without making contact with her. A group of nine members meet once a week to play Mexican Train Dominoes (a game mother always liked to play), and they have included her in the game. She has to have help playing now, but they patiently wait for her, showing her what to play, if necessary. Thanks, again, for these particular thoughts that relate to Alzheimer's with a member of God's Kingdom."

Another person added a comment: "I have always had poor memory - my father called it 'selective memory.' I find mine actually improving with age. Maybe what is important to me is changing. Remember, dementia is not forgetting where you left your keys, it is forgetting what the keys are for! A former Pastor was of great help to me when I was caring for my mother who died of Alzheimer's. In fact, the entire congregation provided spiritual and emotional support for us."

It is encouraging to read these testimonials. The Biblical Church can and must be able to show greater patience, understanding, kindness, acceptance and appreciation for one of its own? There is no suggestion that dementia or Alzheimer's can be reversed. The person experiencing this mental transition is frustrated inwardly – wanting to remember dates and details – but no longer capable to do so.

When a person reaches that point, those who still have some degree of soundness of mind need to always be considerate and in a compassionate mode. The hope and prayer is that we can and will do what we can to embrace that brother and sister in Christ who is struggling with a failing mind. They will benefit greatly from being included and valued. Prayerfully – consider these things with me! We should help those who are helpless or slowly becoming mentally diminished. May the Lord enable each of us to faithfully do so.

To Remember:

To be all things to all people is not always easy
but it is the way the Master is best served
and what He would have us do.

5. Memory and Memorization

Perspective and Reality Moment

In Chapter 4, reference was made to dementia and/or forgetfulness. Dementia is an inner condition that one cannot control. The person so affected tries to navigate with the frustration of knowing and remembering, and the context of how or why there is increasingly frequent forgetfulness. When this occurs with a person, family members and friends should be sensitive to that condition and "fill in the blanks" for the individual. If one is struggling to remember another's name, that person ought to lovingly, gently and kindly (and with a smile) remind one what their name is: "Hi! I'm Jim. How are you today?" All of us must understand the frustration and struggle for the one whose memory is failing or faltering. The task is simple enough. Romans 15:1-7 (NIV – Selected) is one basic approach: "We who are strong ought to bear with the failings of the weak... Each of us should please our neighbors for their good, to build them up... Accept one another just as Christ accepted you..." All of us are capable of implementing this basic consideration.

One suggested and possible preventative to total memory loss may be the practice of Memorization. One general mnemonic device was utilized in Psalm 119. It served a couple of purposes, not the least of which was the learning and remembering the principles of God's standards and values. The Psalm is structured with 24 sections with each containing 8 verses; each section utilizes a letter of the 24 characters of the Hebrew Alphabet. It was a device to assist people to remember. A key reason given is Psalm 119:11, "I have stored up (treasured, hidden) your word in my heart, that I might not sin against you." Again, in Psalm 119:16, "I will delight in your statutes; I will not forget your word."

Cultivation of the memory while one is young (younger) may serve one well in the aging process as/when "forgetting" becomes more and more present. Two verses that should be cherished are, Proverbs 10:17, "The memory of the righteous is a blessing." And, John 14:26, "The Holy Spirit, whom the Father will send in my name will teach you all things and bring to your remembrance all that I have said to you." The mind is a very complicated part of who a person is and what a person may remember. With aging and the onset of forgetfulness, one of the haunting realities is vague remembrance of the past, especially as it pertains to sins of omission and commission. It would serve us all well if we could saturate our souls with this truth about our Savior, the Lord Jesus Christ, Isaiah 43:25, "I, even I, am he who blots out your transgressions, for my own sake, and remembers your sins no more." May this be a great truth that you personally remember regarding God's love, mercy and grace toward you.

Despite one's failing or faltering situation, they should and need to be encouraged to participate in those things that would uplift them in a positive manner. Sadly, several churches have drifted away from internal social activities. My wife had an Aunt who was featured in a Chattanooga, TN Newspaper as participating in a weekly church quilting group. They highlighted that even at her advanced years (86) she was able to quilt using very fine stitches. When my wife's cousin died, rather than Floral Displays at the Church, there were these beautiful quilts appropriately draped over the Floral Pedestals. They were part of what her aunt and cousins had worked on over the years. Before the Estate Sale liquidated the possessions left behind, my wife and her sister, who were the surviving relatives. Each of our children were able to have one of the quilts so carefully and lovingly done.

There could be and should be other social-type groups within the church ministry where the aging can participate and their faltering and failing memories could be briefly rejuvenated – even if just for a moment. Lifeway Online posted an article: Five Ways To Care For The Aging In Your Congregation. Some of their suggestions include:

First, program around the aged in your church. Create programs targeted for retirees and the older population of your congregation. Consider the aging trends in society by focusing more on connecting older people and their friends. Events such a lunches and special trips appeal to this age group and allow them the opportunity to share in the fellowship of the local church.

Second, provide assistance through younger members. You may find that older congregants need help driving to the doctor or to the grocery store. Arrange partnerships with other members of the church who are willing to help the seniors with these weekly tasks.

Third, the Pastor should preach on topics that are important to the older members. The older members in your church have specific spiritual challenges as they face the sunset of their life. Help them to navigate these challenges.

Fourth, pay attention to their life's story. Those who care about the aged will spend time visiting and listening to the aging ones of their church. Visit and just listen and learn from their life's wisdom. Learn to listen to their story.

Fifth, plan for specific events in their life. Issues such as sickness and death, grief over a lost loved one or rejection from children are events that can be planned for ahead of time. Inquire about family members, or their favorite passage of Scripture or even a favorite song. Many times, too often it seems, the aging members in the church family and congregation feel neglected and forgotten. This should never be allowed and every effort should be made to prevent it from occurring. Prayerfully – consider these things with me.

To Remember:

Be Kind and Considerate to all - always.

6. Remembering

Perspective and Reality Moment

For many years in his life time, Bob Hope would regularly visit the American troops who were away from home. One of the signature moments was at the end of the show, he would sing: Thanks For The Memories. One of the many stanzas that he had written for this song included: "Thanks for the memory of sentimental verse, nothing in my purse, and chuckles when the Preacher said for better or for worse, how lovely it was." ¬¬Memories are an important part of one's life – where he came from; who his relatives were/are; friends from the past; education and employment; positions sought but never attained. It's nice to have Scrap Books, Photo Albums and Videos to look through, view and to reflect upon the memories of the past.

There is no better place to have memories than with one's spiritual growth. I was always intrigued by the fourth commandment (Exodus 20:8-11; Deuteronomy 5:12-15) where one is reminded to "Remember the Sabbath Day to keep it holy." As the years have passed, the application of the word "Remember" has become passé. The word "remember" is so important because too many people are in the habit of forgetting the Sabbath Day as a day for God and treating it as a recreational day for personal pleasures and other matters for themselves.

Another passage where the word "Remember" is significant is Ecclesiastes 12:1, "Remember your Creator in the days of your youth." The point that is made is that one should develop the spiritual relationship and discipline of being focused upon God the Creator. If the habit and commitment is established in one's youth, the concept stated to "Remember" will be ingrained and established within one's body, soul, mind and spirit.

One of the major Biblical truths pertains to The Lamb's Book of Life (Revelation 20:12-15, NIV). Malachi 3:16-18 (NASB) also references a Book of Remembrance: "Then those who feared the Lord spoke to one another, and the Lord gave attention and heard it, and A Book of Remembrance was written before Him for those who fear the Lord and esteem His name." It also speaks of judgment awaiting those who did not fear the Lord and chose a different pathway for their personal choices and journey.

Aside from remembering the Sabbath day to keep it holy, what else is one is supposed to be remembering? An earlier reference to Psalm 119:11,16 indicates a foundation purpose and suggests how remembering and memorization dovetail together. The Alliance Devotional Web Page had these interesting and helpful words written years ago by Dr. A.W. Tozer on the subject: Memorization Priority. They are words that should encourage and challenge each of us to become more saturated with and by God's Word and one's close fellowship with the Lord. He summarized the devotional with these words, thoughts and prayer: "My own method is to confine my memorization to the Scriptures and the great hymns. I memorize passages of Scripture so I can use them in my sermons and meditate on them as I travel. And I like to store the great hymns in my mind to sing under my breath anywhere under any circumstances at any time. Further than that I do not give myself too much concern about memorizing. The Verse is Psalm 119:11, "I have hidden your word in my heart that I might not sin against you." His thought is: "Some of us have minds highly retentive. Then there are others of us with minds like a sieve - perpetual leakage. We must continually learn and relearn. It is hard to hide God's Word in our hearts but it is worth the effort! He adds this Personal Prayer, "Meditating upon Your Word helps me to hide it in my heart. Lord, may I have the good sense to fill my heart with Your Word and that which clarifies it."

One of the purposes of treasuring God's Word in one's heart is that it will serve as an indicator of that which is sin. It will also serve as an insulator preventing one from both folly and carelessness with matters of the soul. Psalm 1:1-2 indicates the subtlety of temptation when ungodliness would seek to ensnare one. The threefold directive in Psalm 1 to prevent one from being beguiled by evil and wickedness is: Walk Not! Stand not! Sit not!

Dr. Tozer's words are helpful and instructive. We need to make it our ambition to emulate that which motivated the servants of God in the past as they sought Him and purposed to do His will regardless of personal cost. With expendable income and increased credit levels, people are more easily enabled to purchase their recreational "toys" that detract and distract. In Luke 14:15-24 (BSB), Jesus shares a parable about the man that planned a great banquet as a celebration. He personally invited friends but they offered an excuse that would prevent them from attending. Luke 14:16-20 (BSB) records that when the Banquet was prepared and ready for the guests who had been invited, they uniformly had devised excuses as to why they were unable to attend. This same type of response occurs in the contemporary culture when an invitation is given to attend a religious event or church dinner.

The excuses of those invited by the Master are lame, inconsiderate and selfish. Those invited just did not want to be bothered. The Master of the household was exasperated, disappointed, and slighted. "He tells his servants: Go out to the highways and the hedges and compel them to come in, so that my house will be full." The idea is to extend the invitation to those who were normally not invited to be a guest at the master's banquet. The Master wants his banquet hall and house filled with dinner guests. The directive to the servants was simple and plain: "Go out to the highways and the hedges and compel them to come in, so that my house will be full." There is also a statement of judgment affixed. Jesus shifts it and makes it applicable to His Second Coming. In doing so, he stated: "For I tell you, not one of those men who were invited will taste my banquet."

How do we treat and respond to the Master's invitation to us and through us? Do we have a sense of urgency when encountering the disenfranchised and those ordinarily overlooked or passed by? Let us remember Who He is and what He has prepared for those whom He has called to be His children. I hope you will prayerfully – consider these things with me. A Hymn penned by Isaac Watts includes these words:

How sweet and awful is the place
with Christ within the doors,
while everlasting love displays
the choicest of her stores.

While all our hearts and all our songs
join to admire the feast,
each of us cries, with thankful tongue,
"Lord, why was I a guest?"

"Why was I made to hear Thy voice,
and enter while there's room,
when thousands make a wretched choice,
and rather starve than come?"

We long to see Thy churches full,
that all the chosen race may,
with one voice and heart and soul,
sing Thy redeeming grace.

To Remember:

God's arms are always ready to indiscriminately
welcome and embrace His people.
He wants His invitation extended enthusiastically to all.
We should never fabricate an excuse for someone else.

7. Memorized or Mesmerized

Perspective and Reality Moment

When one pauses to reflect upon life, all kinds of thoughts come rushing through one's mind. The reflection can be about pleasant memories from the past or, if it was possible, do-over things. It is interesting when discussing the past with one's siblings. My sister and I had great moments when we teased our late brother about some of his embellished stories. He was a great story-teller. Some would sit and be mesmerized (to hypnotize, spellbind, fascinate) as the plots were developed and the story told. A distant relative once asked while we were visiting, "Are these stories true?" Despite the embellishment, there was a thread or two that was true whereas the majority was more fanciful than factual.

When thinking about the positives from the past, there are some lines in the Amy Grant song, Heirlooms, that are very meaningful. She wrote and sang about: "Lifetimes of boxes, Timeless to me. Letters and photographs, yellowed with years, some bringing laughter, some bringing tears. Time never changes, the memories, the faces of loved ones...My precious family is more than an heirloom to me." One cannot help but be touched emotionally as the words and music unfold and amplify that which is far more important personally than the cultural influences and obsessions at a given point in a life cycle. Now that our brother is no longer living, we would love to hear him tell one more of his embellished stories.

On the spiritual plane, there is an important lesson taught and an observance required regarding the institution of the Passover. For Egypt, it would be the enactment of judgment and punishment; for Israel, it would represent deliverance and being spared punishment. Exodus 12:24-27 (NASB) references the duty toward children as Moses states this summary: "And you shall observe this event as an ordinance for you and your children forever. When you enter the land, which the Lord will give you, as He promised, you shall observe this rite (ordinance), And when the children say to you: What does this rite (ordinance) mean to you? You shall say: It is a Passover sacrifice to the Lord who passed over the houses of the sons of Israel in Egypt when He smote the Egyptians, but spared our homes. And the people bowed low and worshipped." A phrase that should not be glossed over is: "What does this rite (ordinance) mean to you?" On a strictly personal basis, what does it mean? Is it just merely a ceremony, ritual, or tradition? Or – is it something far more significant and purposeful for those who are remembering why the Passover was instituted? Paul wrote about it in First Corinthians 5:7-8, and stated, "Christ, our Passover lamb, has been sacrificed."

On another occasion, Memorial Stones would be placed appropriately to remind the people of God's faithfulness and care for His people. Joshua 4:4-7 (NLT) states the purpose: "Joshua called together the twelve men he had chosen—one from each of the tribes of Israel. He told them: Go into the middle of the Jordan, in front of the ark of the Lord your God. Each of you must pick up one stone and carry it out on your shoulder—twelve stones in all, one for each of the twelve tribes of Israel. We will use these stones to build a memorial. In the future, your children will ask you: What do these stones mean? Then you can tell them: They remind us that the Jordan River stopped flowing when the ark of the Lord's covenant went across. These stones will stand as a memorial among the people of Israel forever."

It is profitable to share these remembrances with the children so they will be instructed and reminded that God's faithfulness and care has no limit toward His people. These positives and blessings should be rehearsed time and time again so that they are not forgotten by future generations. A way this could be done is to unite as a family in singing the Hymn: "Great Is Thy Faithfulness." Afterwards, discussion of God's faithfulness, care and provision should occur. It could solicit from the children their personal moments of God's care, provision and blessing for them as an individual and family unit. The refrain of the Hymn contains these words as a united testimony:

> Morning by morning new mercies I see.
> All I have needed Thy hand hath provided;
> Great is Thy faithfulness, Lord, unto me!

To Remember:

God is Always Faithful – He cannot and will not deny Himself.

Prayerfully – consider these things with me

8. Being Fortuitous

Perspective and Reality Moment

Everyone views life through his/her personal prism. We do not exist in a vacuum! We all have our values and biases. However, there are those who believe some "magic" has been at work in their behalf – maybe "karma"! There are numbers of people who believe that everything occurring in life is to be relegated and embraced as "good luck" – a matter of being in the right place at the right time. It is viewed as "chance" (things just happen). One can hear some commentator allude to "having to play the hand you've been dealt." Much of this falls into the areas of relativism (no ideas or beliefs are universally true...their validity depends on the circumstances in which they are applied), and/or fatalism (all things are subject to fate, are predetermined, or that they take place by inevitable necessity). Determinism attaches itself to these views of life by allowing: "... that every state of affairs, including every human event, act, and decision is the inevitable consequence of antecedent states of affairs..." In other words, free will and intelligent choices are inconsequential – things are the way they are because of natural forces that predetermined that's how they would be.

The above views and definitions have serious consequences. All of those views rule out design and order in the universe. It becomes part of the evolutionary school of thought and finds expression through various philosophies in the quest for being and the search for reality. If one's presuppositions disallow for the supernatural, then the quest and search become endless and more and more circular. It becomes impossible to arrive at any foundational reality. In like manner, any attempt to define reality apart from the supernatural causes one to wander in the abyss of incredibility.

On the one hand, Paleontologists focus on "body fossils and trace fossils as the principal types of evidence about ancient life, and geochemical evidence has helped to decipher the (assumed) evolution of life before there were organisms large enough to leave fossils. Estimating the dates of these remains is essential but difficult. Paleontologists have to rely on relative dating by solving the jigsaw puzzles of biostratigraphy (the study of the spatial and temporal distribution of fossil organisms, often interpolated with radiometric, geochemical, and paleo-environmental information as a means of dating rock strata)."

The Psalmist understands origins, life and reality much differently. In Psalm 139:13 through 18, "For you created my inmost being; you knit me together in my mother's womb. I praise you because I am fearfully and wonderfully made; your works are wonderful, I know that full well. My frame was not hidden from you when I was made in the secret place. When I was woven together in the depths of the earth, your eyes saw my unformed body. All the days ordained for me were written in your book before one of them came to be. How precious to me are your thoughts, O God! How vast is the sum of them! If I were I to count them, they would outnumber the grains of sand. When I awake, I am still with you…"

Atheism is a very empty, meaningless and directionless philosophy for life. It is a belief system with a negative viewpoint – no god, no eternity, and no foundational values. Many atheists are very intelligent and well-spoken. It's difficult to understand why they would embrace their views and argue them. Psalm 14:1 allows, "The fool says in his heart: There is no God. They are corrupt, their deeds are vile; there is no one who does good." It goes a step further when James allows that the unseen world has a viewpoint regarding theism – stating that demons believe there is a God and tremble (James 2:19 - NLT). James is stating that speech and practice must intersect and demonstrate that what one believes is evidenced by what one is and does. An old Hymn echoes these thoughts:

"What you are speaks so loud
that the world can't hear what you say;
they're looking at your walk,
not listening to your talk
they're judging from your actions every day.
Don't believe you'll deceive
by claiming what you've never known;
they'll accept what they see and know you to be,
they'll judge from your life alone."
~ Author Unknown ~

Words of wisdom should be cherished and implemented in all areas of one's life. Prayerfully – consider these things with me.

To Remember:
God is seeking people of integrity
and authenticity to represent Him.

9. Absolute Hypothesis

Perspective and Reality Moment

With the world trending toward cultural captivity, it is both incredulous and amazing when one considers that which is deemed a priority by world leaders and representatives. A Headline on CNS News stated: United Nations Climate Chief, Christiana Figueres said: "(We're) not very far from considering climate change as a public health emergency." She repeated her comments when: "(she) told a World Health Organization (WHO) hosted event in Geneva that we are not very far from the point where climate change should be declared an international public health emergency, according to her prepared remarks." In 2014, the United States Secretary of State John Kerry had called climate change "the biggest challenge of all that we face right now," and his French counterpart has warned of climate chaos in 500 days, and now the U.N. climate change chief is implying that climate change can be viewed on a par with the deadly Ebola outbreak. In her speech, Figueres said that while it was easy to view climate change as "the equivalent of a disease" it was actually the "symptom." The disease is something we rarely admit, she said. "The disease is humanity's unhealthy dependence on fossil fuels, deforestation and land use that depletes natural resources."

These leaders and others speak in absolutes regarding global warming. It should be alarming to the citizens of the United States, as well as all other nations, when the U.S. Secretary of State indicated that it is: "the biggest challenge of all that we face right now." One would suppose from that comment that world events have little or no significance in comparison when compared to the absolute hypothesis regarding "humanity's unhealthy dependence on fossil fuels, deforestation and land use that depletes natural resources." Is one supposed to ignore the current world events:

1. Russia's troop movements into Ukraine? Are we supposed to be naive and detached to what the intent is for Russia?

2. ISIS and their growing radical military capability in Iraq, Syria, Lebanon and anywhere else they decide to make their objectives and presence known?

3. The persecution of non-Islamists in the Middle East, as well as the genocide there and elsewhere in the world? Economic uncertainty in the United States and other key nations of the world?

4. The Leadership vacuum and the lack of a strategy for combatting a great evil being perpetrated in the Middle East with no credible opposition?

5. The steady erosion of religious influence and impact in our nation and world?

6. The porous border that allows illegal immigrants easy entrance into the nation and claiming eligibility for government assistance through various welfare subsidies?

The champions of the absolute hypothesis are engaged in seeking agreements that will enable them to impose their mandates upon the citizens of the world. The CNS Report continued:

9. Absolute Hypothesis

"The United Nations Secretary-General Ban Ki-moon will host a summit in New York where world leaders will be urged to make commitments ahead of the Paris conference. This agreement will be universal and applicable to all countries. It will address current and future emissions. If strong enough, it will prevent the worst and chart a course toward a world with clean air and water, abundant natural resources and happy, healthy populations, all the requirements for positive growth. Seen in this light, the climate agreement is actually a public health agreement."

One should be concerned regarding how God views what is happening in His world. There are two possibilities. The first is indicated in Psalm 2,

"Why do the nations conspire and the peoples plot in vain? The kings of the earth take their stand and the rulers gather together against the Lord and against his Anointed One. Let us break their chains, they say, and throw off their fetters. The One enthroned in heaven laughs; the Lord scoffs at them. Then he rebukes them in his anger and terrifies them in his wrath…"

The thought is that God laughs at the folly of mankind as they scurry about the world like ants without any purpose or reason for their behavior or actions.

The second possibility is indicated in Genesis 6, "Then the Lord said: My Spirit will not contend with man forever, for he is mortal…the Lord saw how great man's wickedness on the earth had become, and that every inclination of the thoughts of his heart was only evil all the time. The Lord was grieved that he had made man on the earth, and his heart was filled with pain." God mandated a flood that would purge His world from evil and wickedness. In Jeremiah 32, the Lord allowed the

Babylonian Captivity because of the people who had turned their backs to God. The people saw no need for God having an active role in their personal or governmental affairs.

There is a ray of hope in every generation if only there was sense enough to seek it and the Lord Who offers it. Will God laugh at the folly of our leaders? Will He be grieved because of our evil and wicked ways? Will He send us off into captivity until we come to our senses and seek Him? We can escape the cultural captivity and the consequences for our having ignored God. It will require that we seek Him now and turn from our foolish and wicked ways now! We will need to arrive at a point where we see ourselves as God sees and then come before Him to amend the ways of the people and nation. The words of Second Chronicles 7:13-16 will need to be embraced and implemented. It must be done with sincerity, personal commitment and a contrite heart.

> "if my people, who are called by my name, will humble themselves and pray and seek my face and turn from their wicked ways, then I will hear from heaven, and I will forgive their sin and will heal their land…Now my eyes will be open and my ears attentive to the prayers offered in this place…My eyes and my heart will always be there."

To Remember:

Loud voices do not always speak true truth
nor should they be allowed to dominate nor
drown out the timid soul.

Prayerfully - consider these things with me.

10. Approval and Affirmation

Perspective and Reality Moment

A truism is that every person, if given a choice, would choose to be wanted; accepted for who they are; recognized for their worth and value; recipients of approval for the level of their achievement; and affirmed as one who is important and valuable for the contribution they can make or are already making. The measure of a person's worth should never be measured in terms of appearance or intellectual achievement. In terms of the traditional Bell Curve, the majority of people will be found more toward the middle of the curve rather than at the beginning or end of it. In all fields of study, the Bell Curve is sustainable. In Education and referenced test scores, a few students do very well and a few do very poorly. It has been found that most scores are bunched together around the mean score (or apex of the curve).

In professional fields, the same conditions prevail. While the goal of all pursuits should be excellence, the individual participants always strive for approval and affirmation. If that does not occur, performance will wane and stress factors will begin to surface. In order to gain recognition, several studies about athletes and the possibility of their use of performance enhancing drugs have occurred. In other instances, politicians wanting to stand out from the crowd have embellished their biographies, exaggerated their narrative and made unsustainable claims for themselves. In the area of education and the effort to excel, cheating and plagiarism has often taken place. It is strange that the public seems to be impressed by the embellished biography but equally pleased if or when it is debunked.

This type of embellishment also finds entry into the area of religion. Credit for ministry accomplishments are often exaggerated. In the attempt to seem important, it is not unusual for one to resort to name-dropping of well-known people. The assumption is because one has spoken with or been in the company of such a person there will be linkage so that people will think the name-dropper is more significant or equally notable. To get a sense of this, read book promotions or biographical notes about a publication. It will be observable with the frequent use of "I" in what is written.

Applying the Bell Curve to Christian ministry, the studies indicate that 10% of a congregation will be loyal to a Minister regardless of any idiosyncrasies he may have; 10% will hold him in low esteem and with disregard; and the 80% are similar to a jury withholding judgment or assessment until or unless he proves himself to be acceptable. Meanwhile, the minister has to strive to please those who have been non-receptive. Is it any wonder that churches tend to shrink in size? The numbers of the 'Nones' (those who want no further part of the control and forms such as creeds and rituals, seek some other alternative) and the 'Dones' (those who bail out of organized churches and want nothing more to do with it) are steadily increasing! Additionally, churches reach an unsustainable point when programs dominate mission; ministers become laden with stress and their family is impacted and often they just give up and go into some other occupation.

What is the valid measure for ministry? First Timothy 4:12-16 indicates: "Don't let anyone look down on you because you are young, but set an example for the believers in speech, in conduct, in love, in faith and in purity...devote yourself to the public reading of Scripture, to preaching and to teaching. Do not neglect your gift, which was given you through prophecy when the body of elders laid their hands on you. Be diligent in these matters; give yourself wholly to them, so that everyone may see your progress. Watch your life and doctrine closely. Persevere in them, because if you do, you will save both yourself and your hearers." If the servant of the Lord follows the Lord wholeheartedly, he will receive the Lord's approval and affirmation (Take note of Joshua 14:6-13). The well-intentioned naysayers in the church will receive their just reward for their words, deeds and actions, as well as their inactions, in the Lord's own time.

To Remember:

Approval by God should always be first
and foremost in the heart of His people.
The way to receive His approval is
to follow the Lord wholeheartedly.

Prayerfully - consider these things with me.

11. Personal Significance

Perspective and Reality Moment

Living out one's life in the contemporary world can become very competitive. Having goals is one thing whereas desiring to be the most recognized, who is viewed as being superior to all others and well-connected is another. Joseph Stowell wrote in Get More Strength For The Journey, August 10, 2017:

> "Modern counseling and psychology focus a lot of attention on obsessive behaviors—whether it's an obsession with food, tobacco, alcohol, pornography, drugs, or even work. But perhaps one of the most overlooked addictions is our obsession with personal significance. Think about the amount of time and energy you spend in maintaining, advancing, expanding, and protecting your sense of significance - making yourself look good, staying on top of the heap, protecting your ego, and living to be more successful than the next guy…We need to face up to the reality that the search for significance is a treacherous pursuit personally. Count the costs. Significance is often gained at the expense of our character as we are willing to lie and cut ethical corners to be viewed well by others."

Envy and jealousy are real issues. Failure to appreciate another person who has greater skill sets is another factor. Thinking of another individual as being lesser rather than greater is too often chronic. For the professing or biblical Christian, it becomes too easy to omit, overlook, ignore or purposely forget Philippians 2:3-4 (NIV), "Do nothing out of selfish ambition or empty pride, but in humility consider others more important than yourselves. Each of you should look not only to your own interests, but also to the interests of others." Two of the negatives that stand out are "selfish ambition" and "empty pride"; whereas "humility" is either feigned or ignored and not even considered. A discipline of life that must be pursued is set forth in First Peter 5:4-6 (NLT), "All of you, serve each other in humility, because God opposes the proud but favors the humble. So, humble yourselves under the mighty power of God, and at the right time he will lift you up in honor." In Proverbs 3:34, we are reminded, "The Lord…is gracious to the humble."

A story is told of a Pastor/Preacher who believed he had done exceptionally well as he delivered a Worship Sermon/Homily. On his way home, he turned to his wife and asked: "How many great preachers are there in the world today?" She wisely responded: "One less than you're thinking about right now!" Facebook can be an interesting place to observe some writing, opining, and thinking of Pastor/Preacher people. It seems some have to be always right and refuse to accept the input of others graciously. Some have responded with sarcasm or remarks of disdain. These are people who should be unfriended, unfollowed, or blocked. Exposure to the egoist or overbearing is non-edifying. There is little to no spiritual benefit from one's suffering fools. We need to remind ourselves frequently of the words in Micah 6:8 (NLT), "This is what the Lord requires of you: to do what is right, to love mercy, and to walk humbly with your God." This is as simple and plain as it can be. If this is what the Lord requires, where is there room for alteration or argument. One either complies or disobeys. Are you one who is complying? Can it be said of you that you are walking humbly with your God? Is it provable and true? Prayerfully – consider these things with me.

11. Personal Significance

To Remember:

God will bring low those
with a haughty spirit.
Proverbs 16:18

12. Being Serious

Perspective and Reality Moment

Are we committed to and in the habit of taking a serious God seriously? In an account of the Church in France during World War II, there were many who were willing to take risks and accept the consequences on the basis of taking a serious God seriously. The author of this brief history is Fred Trost. A conclusion he emphasized repeatedly was:

> "Taking the Bible seriously is not a program of some kind. It is not a curriculum. It is not a directive from some source far away. It is not a strategy to solve our problems. It is not a suggestion easily made. It has consequences. It is the simple act of faithful people, done for generations, sometimes at a risk, enabling the Church to make its way through time and events with a song on its lips, often in the face of the laughter and derision of the world. The reality is hammer blows are struck from time to time. This belongs to taking the Bible seriously."

We need to be practical and serious about the Word of God and what we believe based upon it. It is not a determination of one's subscription to creeds or rituals. It is the practical application of God's Word to our lives and real life situations. For instance, what do you believe the words in Proverbs 31:8-9 mean and how one should apply them: "Speak up for those who cannot speak for themselves, for the rights of all who are destitute. Speak up and judge fairly; defend the rights of the poor and needy." Is this what you regularly and seriously do? In what way? About what issues?

In 2011, a book I authored was published. The title is: *Taking A Serious God Seriously*. It points out how malaise and detachment have taken over the way life is viewed and what responsibility one has to seek a reversal of the trends. In the book, seven national crimes were listed that apply to both the culture and the church. They give explanation to why things are the way they are: (1) I don't think; (2) I don't know; (3) I don't care; (4) I'm too busy; (5) I leave well enough alone; (6) I have no time to read and find out; (7) I'm not interested."

How far reaching is that mindset when it comes to religion? Another place where seriousness about God and His desire is sometimes lacking is given in Matthew 5 through 7 when Jesus gave His Sermon on the Mount. The Beatitudes beautifully express the pathway for blessing for those who take His words seriously. One beatitude states (Matthew 5:6): "Blessed are those who hunger and thirst after righteousness for they shall be filled." How many know the pangs of hunger and the parching due to thirst? In his devotional thoughts on God Hunger, Dr. A.W. Tozer stated:

> "Hunger is a pain. It is God's merciful provision, a divinely sent stimulus to propel us in the direction of food. If food-hunger is a pain, thirst, which is water-hunger, is a hundredfold worse, and the more critical the need becomes within the living organism the more acute the pain. It is nature's last drastic effort to rouse the imperiled life to seek to renew itself."

The spiritual application is clear and obvious. Is this the way we seek after God and His righteousness? Preachers preach it but don't do it; parishioners read it but fail to apply it; denominations claim it but don't fully embrace it.

As the forces of darkness gain a greater foothold in the world and culture, the serious biblical Christian is to live out the words of Jesus Christ (Matthew 5:13-14): "You are the salt of the earth...You are the light of the world." Have we applied these words of a serious Jesus seriously? Are these truths defining who we are and the basis for what we do? Are we seen in our world as both salt and light as we declare and reflect who Jesus is? Questions that should be asked and responded to frequently are: If not now – when? If not here – where? When and how will one begin to take a serious God seriously? In 1940, Herbert Buffum, Jr. wrote a Hymn: "Everybody Ought to Know." It was popularized more by its refrain that was sung in Bible Conferences as a "round" and participation chorus. The basic Lyric is:

> Everybody ought to know
> (echo: Everybody ought to know)
> Who Jesus is. (echo: Who Jesus is).
> He's the Lily of the Valley.
> He's the Bright and Morning Star.
> He's the Fairest of Ten thousand.
> Everybody ought to know.

These are words that deserve to be remembered. Prayerfully – consider these things with me.

To Remember:

God is totally serious about whether or not
His followers are taking Him seriously.
The Lord reminded His people:
You will seek Me and find Me
when you search for Me with all your heart.
I will be found by you, declares the Lord,
and I will restore you...
~ Jeremiah 29:13-14 (NASB) ~

13. Souls in Anguish

Perspective and Reality Moment

On November 30, 2007, a troubled man in Rochester, New Hampshire held several people hostage in a Political Campaign Office. It was commendable that no physical harm was done to anyone. What caused this man to take this drastic action? Why did he indicate he would blow himself up? What issues provoked his behavior? In a telephone call to CNN, he indicated he had mental health needs that required attention and he wasn't able to get the help he needed. In this strange incident, this depressed man seems to have been crying out for help and was being ignored by those who could give it. He claimed this was the sole cause for his threatening and menacing behavior.

Mental health matters impact many people, especially during the holidays, and should always be a concern and understood by others. For the person with mental health issue and dysfunction, such times may evoke loneliness; reflection upon failures of the past; loss of loved ones; rehearsal of missed opportunities.

Even within the professional ranks, depression is a reality. A study by the Mental Health Administration (2004-2006) found that nearly two out of ten who serve in the personal care and service profession reported being depressed. Major depression strikes 17 percent of Americans and government figures show about 30,000 a year commit suicide, according to USA Today.

My Grandmother Isabella would remind us often when she used the phrase about people of different walks and backgrounds: "They are more to be pitied than laughed at!" In the rush of our lives and the multitude of our activities, we need to notice others around us and give due consideration to those we might deem to be dysfunctional, a person with complex issues, or even one who is a bit "weird"! Those who honor Jesus Christ as Savior and Lord would do well to remember the Scriptures that touch on these areas that impacts different ones: (Psalm 34:18), "The Lord is close to the broken hearted and saves those who are crushed in spirit." (Proverbs 17:22), "A cheerful heart is good medicine, but a crushed spirit dries up the bones." (Second Corinthians 4:8), "We are hard pressed on every side, but not crushed: perplexed but not in despair."

Whether we say "Merry Christmas" or "Happy Holidays", for some of our acquaintances and neighbors, it is anything but a merry or happy time. This would be true for the one struggling through personal mental health concerns. We need to be deliberate in doing our part to lift up the troubled spirit and to help bear the burden of the troubled soul. Sometimes, those who need the assistance and help the most will reject your effort and offer. But – keep on trying! You may be the only one who demonstrates care! Don't give up! Do what you can to have a positive thrust into another's life. It could be a life or death struggle that you have helped to avert. Represent that you are motivated by doing this in Jesus name. Share with them in action and behavior that which the one with mental health concerns can embrace. Three Biblical passages to reference: First, Psalm 55:22 – Cast your burden upon the Lord and He will sustain you. Second, First Peter 5:7 – Casting all of your care upon Him, because He cares for you. Third, Matthew 6:25-34 (BSB) – especially verses 31 and 33 - where Jesus Christ assures His followers: Do not worry, saying: What shall we eat? or What shall we drink? or What shall we wear? …Your Heavenly Father knows that you need them. But seek first the kingdom of God and His righteousness, and all these things will be added unto you.

13. Souls in Anguish

Souls in anguish need to remember the words written in 1932 by Charles Weigle:

> No one ever cared for me like Jesus;
> There's no other friend so kind as He.
> No one else could take the sin and darkness from me;
> O how much He cared for me.

Prayerfully – consider these things with me.

To Remember:

God always cares for His own.
Give Him all your anxieties,
all your burdens, and
all your cares.

14. Sense of Being Powerless

Perspective and Reality Moment

In theology, a term used about God is that He alone is Omnipotent – all-powerful. In practical application, it is amazing how often that reality is forgotten. It has nothing to do with God's ability to display His power, it has everything to do with our faith to believe that "our God is able...and He will" (Daniel 3:16-18 - NASB). God's power cannot be diminished by man's resistance.

Second Chronicles 20:5-13 contains a public prayer by King Jehoshaphat. He recognizes God's power in terms of the past but expresses his concern about what God's power can or will be in the present. He prays:

> "Lord, the God of our ancestors, are you not the God who is in heaven? You rule over all the kingdoms of the nations. Power and might are in your hand, and no one can withstand you...But now here are men from Ammon, Moab and Mount Seir...Our God, will you not judge them? For we have no power to face this vast army that is attacking us. We do not know what to do, but our eyes are on you. All the men of Judah, with their wives and children and little ones, stood there before the Lord."

Two additional verses of Scripture regarding God's available power in and for us that should be part of our conviction and confidence are: First, the words of our relationship to God in Christ. In Second Peter 1:3, "His divine power has given us everything we need for a godly life through our knowledge of him who called us by his own glory and goodness." Second, is a verse that will test the measure of one's faith and hope. Ephesians 3:20, "Now to him who is able to do immeasurably more than all we ask or imagine, according to His power that is at work within us..."

Don't be focused on personal weaknesses but focus on God's strength and power. Don't look at your situations and circumstances with helplessness and hopelessness but look to His power that is in you to do immeasurably more than you can ask of imagine. Prayerfully –consider these things with me.

To Remember:

Our God power is never inadequate.
He is always all-powerful.
He is never prevented from accomplishing
all His will in one's behalf.

15. Procrastination

Perspective and Reality Moment

For some time, I've been wanting to write about the subject of Procrastination but have never gotten around to doing it! I've always thought there would be a better day, time or place for doing it. However, we'll have to see how far I can get before deciding that I'll finish these remarks another time. There was something I promised myself that I'd do yesterday and didn't get done. Actually, I never got started on it, so I better get that done before I continue writing about Procrastination. The proverb that states: "Never put off to tomorrow what you can do today!" finds no entrance into the thought processes of a typical Procrastinator. Some have gone so far as to organize and become a Group of Procrastinators.

A man – Robert C. Shannon – wrote: "There really is a Procrastinators' Club of America, with headquarters in Philadelphia, PA. Their objective is to make known the benefits of putting things off until later. They publish last month's newsletter, and have protested against the War of 1812; tried to get someone to fix the crack in the Liberty Bell; and traveled to Spain to try to raise money for three ships to discover America. The club holds irregular and, of course, late, meetings. If all of us who put things off were to join, it would be the biggest organization in the world. No doubt many of us intend to join, we just haven't gotten around to it yet!" Someone (unknown) wrote a Poem that gives some sense and insight to how the procrastinator thinks:

I spent a fortune on a trampoline, a stationary bike and a rowing machine complete with gadgets to read my pulse, and gadgets to prove my progress results, and others to show the miles I've charted – but they left off the gadget to get me started!

That's a sad picture and story about too many of us. Some pithy and humorous comments regarding Procrastination are:

- "Only Robinson Crusoe had everything done by Friday."
- "The sooner I fall behind, the more time I have to catch up."
- "If it weren't for the last minute, I wouldn't get anything done."
- "Some-day is not a day of the week."

With that in mind, there is this statement in Proverbs 27:1 (ESV), "Do not boast about tomorrow, for you do not know what a day may bring." In the Message Paraphrase: "Don't brashly announce what you're going to do tomorrow; you don't know the first thing about tomorrow." That is just as clear and plain as it gets. One must take care of matters today. No one can predict whether or not there will be a tomorrow in one's lifespan. Psalm 90:10-12 states: "The length of our days is seventy years - or eighty, if we have the strength; yet their span is but trouble and sorrow, for they quickly pass, and we fly away…Teach us to number our days aright, that we may gain a heart of wisdom."

There is a positive commitment and discipline if one is to overcome the innate desire to put things off to another time and place, that is, to procrastinate. Psalm 119:57-61 shares these words as an antidote to the tendency to procrastinate: "You are my portion, O Lord; I have promised to obey your words. I have sought your face with all my heart; be gracious to me according to your promise. I have considered my ways and have turned my steps to your statutes. I will hasten and not delay to obey your commands…I will not forget your law."

15. Procrastination

Do you see the seven steps given by the Psalmist? They are:

1) I have promised to obey;
2) I have sought Your face;
3) I have considered my ways;
4) I have turned my steps to Your Statutes;
5) I will hasten;
6) I will not delay;
7) I will not forget Your Law.

Jesus addressed the perils associated with procrastination in Luke 9:57-62, "As they were walking along the road, a man said to him, I will follow you wherever you go...He said to another man, Follow me. But the man replied, Lord, first let me go and bury my father. Jesus said to him, Let the dead bury their own dead, but you go and proclaim the kingdom of God. Still another said, I will follow you, Lord; but first let me go back and say good-by to my family. Jesus replied, No one who puts his hand to the plow and looks back is fit for service in the kingdom of God."

All kinds of distractions arise. Some are valid whereas others are invalid. One's "to-do" list can become longer and distract one further from getting to do anything on the list. Focus on other choices and priorities is also procrastination. Staying focused and committed are two significant traits of Christian character. We should consistently attempt to consider these things that Jesus said and taught! It will develop discipline and spiritual growth in one's life. Galatians 5 addresses the distractions of the flesh versus the growth and development of the fruit of the Spirit within one. Two verses in this Chapter serve as an ongoing personal instruction. Galatians 5:16 and 5:25, "Walk by the Spirit (by His enablement), and you will not gratify the desires of the flesh...Since we live by the Spirit, let us walk in step

59

(marching with precision) with the Spirit." Don't procrastinate! Just do it!

There is a poem for people wanting hope. The title is: "Yesterday, Today and Tomorrow." It is read in many 12-step meetings around the world:

Yesterday Today and Tomorrow.

There are two days in every week about which we should not worry, Two days which should be kept free of fear and apprehension.

One of these days is yesterday, With its mistakes and cares, Its faults and blunders, Its aches and pains. Yesterday has passed forever beyond our control.

All the money in the world cannot bring back yesterday. We cannot undo a single act we performed; we cannot erase a single word we said. Yesterday is gone.

The other day we should not worry about is tomorrow, with its possible adversities, its burdens, its larger promise. Tomorrow is also beyond our immediate control.

Tomorrow, the sun will rise, either in splendor or behind a mask of clouds, but it will rise. Until it does, we have no stake in tomorrow for it is as yet unborn.

This leaves only one day – today. Any man can fight the battles of just one day. It is only when you and I add
the burdens of those two awful eternities – yesterday and tomorrow – That we break down.

It is not the experience of today that drives men mad. It is remorse or bitterness for something which happened yesterday. And the dread of what tomorrow may bring.

Let us, therefore, live but one day at a time.

Prayerfully - consider these things with me.

To Remember:

Today is the Tomorrow
we spoke about Yesterday.

16. Transitions

Perspective and Reality Moment

One of the more difficult moments in life is when transitions occur. Some can be planned for in advance, whereas others occur due to events and decisions without warning or time to prepare for them. In recent months, we have shared in the times of sorrow with those whose spouse either suddenly died or became afflicted with a malady for which there was little or no remedy. In other instances, there have been those who have experienced transition with their employment. This is especially trying and difficult if/when it occurs with one who has been called to serve the Lord as a Missionary or as a Minister/Pastor for whom the call resulted in a life-time commitment. Such a transition is borderline traumatic.

Countless numbers of Missionaries are trying to accomplish ministry in the so-called "hot spots" of our world. They are desirous of continuing their ministry. It has been their calling and they have sacrificed to be where they believe the Lord wants them to be. The Geo-Political times in which we are living will determine whether or not the Missionary effort can continue in places where radical Islam is on the move and anything "Christian" is viewed as anathema. Anyone who identifies as being a Christian and is attached to such a group will be removed or put to death. The Coptic Church in Egypt and the Assyrian Christians in Iraq (Mosul) are just two illustrations of groups under attack.

I think of Pastors who are no longer viewed as viable in various church situations. A spiritual work falls under a secular-type assessment and the Minister/Pastor is viewed as expendable. In a more humane, although devastating way, he is asked to leave or is prevented from continuing in his calling in a local church situation. Over the years, as and when this has taken place, the desired result that was anticipated did not occur. These type things, while reported as being unanimous, seldom are to the liking and support of all the people. The church will either stay as it has been, continue to move sideways with little or no appreciable change, or the worst scenario - it will begin to drift downward and people will no longer faithfully attend.

Barna Research Group reports the following (Spring 2014): "In America, 3500-4000 churches close their doors each year. Churches lose an estimated 2,765,000 people each year to nominalism and secularism." From Religious Tolerance, this report: "Only 21% of Americans attend religious services every week." The drift downward in church attendance can be seen in an older report by the Church Society: "Usual Sunday church attendance has dropped from 1,606,000 in 1968 to 881,000 in 2005." This trend continues to this day. Another sad fact reported is: "Since 2010, 270 churches have been sold after defaulting on their loans, with 90 percent of those sales coming after a lender-triggered foreclosure, according to the real estate information company Co-Star Group."

When my wife and I committed ourselves to ministry, we had originally applied to go to China. Certain factors prevented that but the commitment level remained constant to go anywhere, to do any work/task, at any time, and at any cost. Psalm 37:4-5,7 was especially significant for us:

> "Delight yourself in the Lord, and he will give you the desires of your heart. Commit your way to the Lord; trust in him, and he will act...Be still before the Lord and wait patiently for him."

Now in our latter years, the words in Psalm 37:25-26 have become an increasing reality and testimony to the faithfulness of God:

"I have been young, and now am old, yet I have not seen the righteous forsaken or his children begging for bread. He is ever lending generously, and his children become a blessing."

We have experienced transitions that have occurred over the years, some of them were painful and confusing. We were concerned for our children as they witnessed carnal behavior on the part of those who were alleged to be "spiritual leaders" in the church. Jesus cautioned about the danger when adults fail to consider the welfare of the little ones among them. In Matthew 18:5-6 (BSB), "And whoever welcomes a little child like this in My name welcomes Me. But if anyone causes one of these little ones who believe in Me to stumble, it would be better for him to have a large millstone hung around his neck and to be drowned in the depths of the sea." God views all of what is occurring in the visible Church and He is not always pleased about what He observes. A sense of what Jesus takes note of is chronicled in Revelation 1-3. To the seven churches discussed, Jesus makes the statement: "I know."

In the course of personal transitions, we are thankful that we and our children were kept from bitterness by the grace of God. There was a day when I gathered our children to share with them that I was sorry for our moving once again and going to serve in another small church. I wanted to indicate my sensitivity toward them having to adjust to a new school and making of new friends. Our oldest child interrupted to say: "Dad – small churches need good Pastors too."

In like manner, it made me think about when transitions occur in your life or ministry commitment. My hope and prayer is that you will lean on the everlasting arms of the one

who knows and cares about you. Prayerfully - consider these
things with me.

To Remember:

Keep looking unto Jesus
at all times and in all circumstances.
He alone is the author and
completer of your faith.

17. Irresolute Resolve

Perspective and Reality Moment

Time has a way of passing rapidly and a new year quickly dawns. A benefit of a new year is that it allows one an opportunity to review the accomplishments of the past year and the continuing aspirations in the new year. Goals and plans are commendable if they are conjoined with motivation, determination, purpose and commitment. The title of this chapter is obviously an oxymoron (a combination of words that have opposite or very different meanings). If or when a person is irresolute, it is because of a hesitancy to press forward with a goal or task. It becomes too easy to second-guess a resolve, direction or proposal. One becomes uncertain in terms of an action or whether to proceed at all. Sir Walter Scott is alleged to have said: "To the timid and hesitating everything is impossible because it seems so." However, there are times and events when it is advisable to pause and to measure the cost and likelihood of success before proceeding. Golda Meir is alleged to have reflected: "A Leader who doesn't hesitate before he sends his nation into battle is not fit to be a leader." A reckless "leader" is a considerable risk to himself and the world.

Almost everyone alive has made some resolution of some sort at some time in terms of a worthy goal or purpose. That which stands between success and failure is commitment and discipline. An uncommitted and/or undisciplined individual will inevitably experience more failures than successes. It may not have anything to do with one's abilities or skill-sets. It is the self-imposed follow-through that will result in achievement. John Maxwell is one of the most outstanding speakers on the subject of Leadership. One of his emphases regarding success is: "Competence goes beyond words. It's the leader's ability to say it, plan it, and do it in such a way that others know that you know how – and know that they want to follow you."

Note the emphasis on the word competence. The loftiest ideals and goals can never be fully attained if one lacks the competence to accomplish them. He also offers this sage advice: "A man must be big enough to admit his mistakes, smart enough to profit from them, and strong enough to correct them."

The Bible contains some great illustrations of resolve. In Joshua 24:14-15, Joshua lays before the people the obvious choice they should make. Regardless of their choice, Joshua states his unequivocal commitment, purpose and resolve: "Now therefore fear the Lord and serve Him in sincerity and in faithfulness…choose this day whom you will serve…But as for me and my house, we will serve the Lord."

In Matthew 6:24, as Jesus is preaching/teaching His Sermon on the Mount, He lays before His disciples and followers a necessary choice in terms of faith and practice: "No one can serve two masters, for either he will hate the one and love the other, or he will be devoted to the one and despise the other. You cannot serve God and money." The matter of choice and decision is an absolute stated by Jesus and it demands and calls for commitment, purpose and resolve – it is either God or someone/something else.

The Apostle Paul faced the considerations and priorities for his life and stated them in Philippians 3:12-14. He has previously stated his strong desire to know Christ in the greatest way possible. He then adds: "Not that I have already obtained this or am already perfect, but I press on to make it my own, because Christ Jesus has made me His own…But one thing I do: forgetting what lies behind and straining forward to what lies ahead, I press on toward the goal for the prize of the upward call of God in Christ Jesus." He states his determination and voices the necessary discipline to attain this most worthy goal.

The Apostle Paul also states the criteria for each one who professes to be a follower of Jesus Christ. In First Thessalonians 5:12-24 he lists 15 goals and commitments one should be willing to establish for his/her life:

(1) respect those who work hard among you, who are over you in the Lord and who admonish you. Hold them in the highest regard in love because of their work.

(2) live in peace with each other.

(3) warn those who are idle,

(4) encourage the timid,

(5) help the weak,

(6) be patient with everyone.

(7) make sure that nobody pays back wrong for wrong, but always try to be kind to each other and to everyone else.

(8) be joyful always;

(9) pray continually (without ceasing);

(10) give thanks in all circumstances, for this is God's will for you in Christ Jesus.

(11) do not put out (quench) the Spirit's fire;

(12) do not treat prophecies with contempt.

(13) test everything.

(14) hold on to the good.

(15) avoid every kind of evil.

Are these goals attainable? To determine whether or not they are achievable, you need to be willing to take these steps on your journey along the narrow way. Set these things as your personal goal, ambition, commitment and discipline. May God richly bless you. Prayerfully - consider these things with me.

To Remember:

Discipline and determination
will enable you to achieve your goals
in Christ Alone.

18. Bamboozled

Perspective and Reality Moment

The culture of the world loves to rest on its status and think it has arrived at a place where it is the most intelligent; the most ingenious; the most capable; the most self-sufficient; the most important people in all human history. While it is true that there have been considerable advances in many important fields of study such as technology, electronics, medicine, science, etc., there are other basic areas where our nation has faltered. A major place to focus would be the education levels within our nation. Studies on public education show a consistent and persistent diminished level in mathematics, science, and reading skills.

Those who conduct these studies come to the table with their presuppositions: ethnic and racial groups will perform poorly, and socio-economic factors contribute greatly to under-performance. One study concludes:

"Achievement disparities are often attributed to socio-economic factors. According to 2009 data from the Census Bureau, of all children younger than 18 living in families, 15.5 million live in poverty...According to a seminal study of language development in 1995, by age 3, children in poverty have smaller vocabularies and lower language skills than children from middle-income families. Research has also shown that dropout rates tend to be higher for children who live in poverty. According to the U.S. Department of Education's 2011 Condition of Education report, about 68 percent of 12th-graders in high-poverty schools graduated with a diploma in 2008, compared with 91 percent of 12th-graders in low-poverty schools. A recent study by the Annie E. Casey Foundation (2011) found that children who both live in poverty and read below grade level by 3rd grade are three times as likely to not graduate from high school…"

Are the above references the actual cause for under-performance or are we being bamboozled (easily deceived)? Synonyms for the word are telling. Bamboozled is parallel with: "gyp, dupe, trick, cheat, swindle, defraud, flimflam, hoax, delude, mislead, fool." One consideration that should be factored in for any study of performance and/or under-performance should be the home and family. There are questions that should be asked and conclusions drawn from the responses. One of the key factors that is impacting the culture is in terms of the family. There is a growing dysfunction in the focus on home and family. In too many instances, child neglect and abuse are accepted as the trend of the times. Few secular solutions surface to alleviate this condition.

This reality should gain primary attention and care. Questions, such as: Does the home of any socio-economic group have a loving and caring Mother and Father who are supportive of a child's educational achievement? Does such a home nurture the child in terms of social activity, Christian religious participation and educational achievement? Does the home and family provide motivation for the child to learn and to take pride in excellence and performance? If these and other matters are not part of the equation, then one is being bamboozled. One of the more important decisions made within the bamboozled trend and process was the diminishing of prayer, bible reading and religious exercises (such as The National Day of Prayer) as being essential for the betterment of the individual child, adult and the nation. Once the emphasis on cultural pluralism emerged, the place for God, prayer and the Bible faded. Pluralism means: "a condition in which minority groups participate fully in the dominant society, yet maintain their cultural differences; a doctrine that a society benefits from such a condition." The mantra became: offend no one - everyone is equal. There is a dynamic that should be considered and examined to determine why home schooling is achieving far more than public education.

This nation and culture needs to give attention to Isaiah 46:8-13 (ESV - Selected), "Remember this and...recall it to mind...I am God, and there is no other; I am God, and there is none like me, declaring the end from the beginning and from ancient times things not yet done, saying: My counsel shall stand, and I will accomplish all my purpose...Listen to me, you stubborn of heart, you who are far from righteousness. I bring near my righteousness and my salvation will not delay..." If our nation had a fraction of the intelligence and common sense about which we boast, we would flee from being bamboozled and return to the Creator of the universe, the Almighty and Eternal God. Our nation also needs to implement Isaiah 55:6-7, "Seek the Lord while he may be found; call upon him while he is near; let the wicked forsake his way, and the unrighteous man his thoughts; let him return to the Lord, that he may have compassion on him, and to our God, for he will abundantly pardon." This raises additional questions that need to be asked and responses that need to be considered: How long do you believe God should wait for His people to seek Him? Equally, how long do you believe God should wait for His people to call upon Him? Is there evidence or viable examples of the wicked forsaking his way and the unrighteous man his thoughts? How long should the Lord wait with His abundant compassion and blessing? How long should one wait with a viable expectation for the Lord's abundant pardon to become a reality?

Review these areas above – carefully - and ask the Lord to help you understand His perspective in these matters. Prayerfully –consider these things with me.

To Remember:

Action now is essential whereas
further delay is will erode and decimate.

19. Multiple Impressions

Perspective and Reality Moment

There is considerable merit in the expression: "You only get one chance to make a good first impression." One thing to remember about multiple impressions is: A chameleon is also capable of making multiple impressions. Suppose a prominent individual begins to have an iconic impact on a growing number of people, should that alone be the basis for a positive impression? Another supposition, what if that person seems to be an egomaniac personality, does that mean he should receive special attention and privilege? What if some of his words are designed to manipulate an audience, does that mean he should be voted for and granted power over other people?

During last year's Presidential debate and election, the political male candidate seeking the office of President, who is leading in all of the many polls that are regularly conducted was given a stage where thousands had assembled as an audience. He was also given the national stage as news networks broadcast his stage presentation and the familiar diatribe of self-promotion; belittling any and all competition; parroting a populist theme that gains some applause; and says what he thinks needs to be said to pretend to be what he thinks his audience wants him to be. For instance, in recent appearances, he always manages to hold up a copy of his book, *The Art of The Deal*. Last evening, he said: "This is the best book ever written" - and then quickly added - "except for one other…The Bible."

The review of his book, *The Art of The Deal*, on Amazon indicates the following comments made by the author: "I like thinking big. I always have. To me it's very simple: if you're going to be thinking anyway, you might as well think big…I play it very loose. I don't carry a briefcase. I try not to schedule too many meetings. I leave my door open...I prefer to come to work each day and just see what develops...I always go into a deal anticipating the worst. If you plan for the worst - if you can live with the worst - the good will always take care of itself."

One impression that came through in his rambling comments was his use of the vernacular with his insertion of "hell" in his remarks. It makes an impression only because an ego-driven person seldom thinks of "hell" in terms of death or judgment. It is just a word to make one sound like he's one of the people when in actuality he would have very little need or use for the people except for their vote to elect him.

Can you think of anyone in Biblical History who made similar boasts and comparable impressions? Did he achieve the position and heights of power? What did he do with that position and power? Did he use it to benefit others or to promote himself? In both secular and Biblical History, Nebuchadnezzar, King of Babylon from 605 BC to 562 BC is noted for both his abilities and his ego-driven actions. Secular history records Nebuchadnezzar as a brutal, powerful, and ambitious king. He is mentioned approximately 90 times in Scripture although the summary of his life is contained in Daniel, Chapters 1 through 4.

The impression one is left with about this king is summarized in Daniel 4 after Nebuchadnezzar is given a dream by God. Daniel interpreted the dream for Nebuchadnezzar and informed him that the dream was a warning for the king to humble himself and recognize that his power, wealth, and influence were from God, not of his own making. The king ignored that interpretation and was driven insane for seven years. When the king's sanity was restored, he finally humbled himself before God. In Daniel 4:3, his acknowledgement about God is: "How great are his signs, how mighty his wonders! His kingdom is an everlasting kingdom, and his dominion endures from generation to generation." He went on to declare, verse 37: "Now I, Nebuchadnezzar, praise and extol and honor the King of heaven, for all his works are right and his ways are just; and those who walk in pride he is able to humble."

What he had neglected, and that which all candidates in a given election cycle need to remember is Proverbs 28:1-2 (MSG), "Good leadership is like a channel of water controlled by God; He directs it to whatever ends he chooses. We justify our actions by appearances; God examines our motives." Many words are spoken in political rhetoric and speeches. All too often the multitude of words begins to give a sound of hollowness and meaninglessness. Terminology is used that exaggerates one's skills and ability to achieve desired goals. However, great boasts are not always accompanied by great deeds. James 3:5-8 (BSB) records, "In the same way, the tongue is a small part of the body, but it boasts of great things. Consider how small a spark sets a great forest on fire. The tongue also is a fire, a world of wickedness among the parts of the body. It pollutes the whole person, sets the course of his life on fire, and is itself set on fire by hell. All kinds of animals, birds, reptiles, and creatures of the sea are being tamed and have been tamed by man, but no man can tame the tongue. It is an unruly evil, full of deadly poison." Prayerfully - consider these things with me!

To Remember:

Becoming part of a stampede
is always unwise, dangerous
- and - can be fatal.

20. Unlearned Lessons

Perspective and Reality Moment

The journey along the narrow way can be a lonely pathway. When Jesus mention the narrow way, He indicated, Matthew 7:13-14 (NLT), "You can enter God's Kingdom only through the narrow gate. The gateway to life is very narrow and the road is difficult, and only a few ever find it." The two words that describe the narrow way is that it is "difficult" and only a "few" ever find it. That should never be a deterrent for one to seek, pursue and navigate along it. It brings to mind an old song of encouragement. Some of the lyrics are:

As you travel along on the Jericho Road,
Does the world seem all wrong and heavy your load?
Just bring it to Christ your sins all confess,
On the Jericho Road, your heart He will bless. On the Jericho Road there's room for just two.
No more and no less, just Jesus and you.
Each burden He'll bear each sorrow He'll share,
There's never a care for Jesus is there.

The narrow way may represent the arduous. It may even appear that one is all alone on this journey. It must be remembered that Jesus referenced the "few" who find it. They are traversing that same road with you. Furthermore, the lyrics quoted above remind us that Jesus is always with us and will never forsake anyone who is journeying along that narrow way. The lessons learned from godly parents and biblical instruction will enable one to remain focused on the goal of the journey and to keep one's eyes looking to Jesus (Hebrews 12:2).

As we journey through life, we are in a constant learning process. If one has godly parents, they have followed a balanced pattern of: "Training up a child in the way he should go, and when he is old he will not depart from it" (Proverbs 22:6). The wise and prudent parent will also make use of firm discipline. Part of it will include the understanding and administration of: "Foolishness is bound up in the heart of a child but the rod of correction will drive it far from him" (Proverbs 22:15). In the field of education, it is interesting to note the emphasis on these terms of "training" and the particular field of study as a "discipline." The lesson in these verses is obviously the regularity of training a child and the proper use and administration of discipline.

Another lesson one is to learn is humility. In First Peter 1:5-6, it is clearly stated: "Clothe yourselves, all of you, with humility toward one another, for God opposes the proud but gives grace to the humble. Humble yourselves, therefore, under the mighty hand of God so that at the proper time he may exalt you." The application words are "all of you" are to be engaged in learning and practicing humility.

It is difficult because the natural instinct is to prove one's self by achieving in order to excel and receive acclaim for those achievements. In that process, too often an exaggerated attitude of how significant one really is begins to surface. Pride is allowed to replace humility and self-aggrandizement comes to the forefront and doesn't wait for God's perfect timing in one's life. When this is one's aim and driving force, it will lead to indescribable tensions and anxieties as one pursues the often-elusive acceptance and acclaim from others. In the process, it also misses a valuable lesson Jesus taught in Matthew 11:29, "Take my yoke upon you, and learn from me, for I am gentle and lowly in heart..."

Athletes who have excelled in their respective sports generally share that a lesson not too easily learned is: "Being humble in victory and gracious in defeat." This attitude and mindset was not easy for the disciples of Jesus. The entire pursuit of acclaim and greatness was illustrated during a strange discussion by the disciples. In Mark 9:33-37, their private discussion and focus regarding who among them was the greatest was taking place. They may have been embarrassed or shocked by what happens next: "(Jesus) came to Capernaum. And when He was in the house He asked them: What was it you disputed among yourselves on the road? But they kept silent, for on the road they had disputed among themselves who would be the greatest. And He sat down, called the twelve, and said to them: If anyone desires to be first, he shall be last of all and servant of all. The intensity of their discussion is described as: "They had disputed among themselves who would be the greatest." It makes it sound as though there was arguing and anger among them. This is similar to a moment in Matthew 20:20-22 when the mother of James and John approached Jesus with a request: "The mother of the sons of Zebedee came up to him with her sons, and kneeling before Him...He said to her: What do you want? She said to him: Say that these two sons of mine are to sit, one at your right hand and one at your left, in your kingdom. Jesus answered: You do not know what you are asking." She was attempting to gain an advantage of honor and authority for her sons by having them in positions of special recognition and prestige.

The lessons of servanthood, lowliness and humility are among the most difficult to learn in the Christian life. One of the major considerations for all servants of the Lord is stated succinctly in   Romans 12:2-3 (NLT),

> "Don't copy the behavior and customs of this world, but let God transform you into a new person by changing the way you think. Then you will learn to know God's will for you, which is good and pleasing and perfect. Because of the privilege and authority God

has given me, I give each of you this warning: Don't think you are better than you really are. Be honest in your evaluation of yourselves, measuring yourselves by the faith God has given us."

What was the Apostle Paul's intention when he penned these words? Albert Barnes shared his thoughts about Paul's intent:

"Not to think – means not to over-estimate himself, or to think more of himself than he ought to. The true standard by which we ought to estimate ourselves he immediately adds: This is a caution against pride; and an exhortation not to judge of ourselves by our talents, wealth, or function, but to form another standard of judging of ourselves, by our Christian character. The Romans would probably be in much danger from this quarter. The prevailing habit of judging among them was according to rank, or wealth, or eloquence, or function. While this habit of judging prevailed in the world around them, there was danger that it might also prevail in the church. And the exhortation was that they should not judge of their own characters by the usual modes among people, but by their Christian attainments. There is no sin to which people are more prone than an inordinate self-valuation and pride."

The pattern for one's behavior is summarized in Micah 6:8, "What does the Lord require of you but to do justice, and to love kindness, and to walk humbly with your God?" These words need to be written indelibly in our hearts and minds. Walk humbly in the presence of God. Prayerfully - consider these things with me!

To Remember:

Learn the basic lesson from Jesus
to be meek (gentle) and
lowly (humble) in heart.
Matthew 11:28-30

21. Prayer

Perspective and Reality Moment

What is prayer? How frequently should a biblical Christian pray? What can and should be included in prayer? Is there a safety net for the prayers people pray? One verse that should be prominent in the prayerful person's thinking is Romans 8:26-27 (NIV): "In the same way, the Spirit helps us in our weakness. We do not know what we ought to pray for, but the Spirit himself intercedes for us through wordless groans. And he who searches our hearts knows the mind of the Spirit, because the Spirit intercedes for God's people in accordance with the will of God."

An online dictionary defines prayer as: "A solemn request for help or expression of thanks addressed to God or an object of worship." In CARM (Christian Apologetics and Research Ministry), Matt Slick responds: "Prayer is the practice of the presence of God. It is the place where pride is abandoned, hope is lifted, and supplication is made. Prayer is the place of admitting our need, of adopting humility, and claiming dependence upon God. Prayer is the needful practice of the Christian. Prayer is the exercise of faith and hope. Prayer is the privilege of touching the heart of the Father through the Son of God, Jesus our Lord."

The *Westminster Shorter Catechism* 98 asks and answers: "What is Prayer? Prayer is an offering up of our desires unto God for things agreeable to his will, in the name of Christ, with confession of our sins, and thankful acknowledgment of his mercies." Some of the Biblical reasons attached to this answer include Psalm 62:5-8 (NIV), "Yes, my soul, find rest in God; my hope comes from him. Truly he is my rock and my salvation; he is my fortress, I will not be shaken…He is my mighty rock, my refuge. Trust in him at all times, you people; pour out your hearts to him, for God is our refuge." First John 5:14 assures us, "And this is the confidence that we have before Him: If we ask anything according to His will, He hears us."

How one's prayer is formulated is crucial. What does one believe about prayer and its formulation? What about rituals and repetitions? Are there any limitations or prohibitions when prayer is being offered in Jesus' name? Jesus indicated, John 16:23-24 (BSB), "Truly, I tell you, whatever you ask the Father in My name, He will give you. Until now you have not asked for anything in My name. Ask and you will receive, so that your joy may be complete."

Is this how your prayer is formulated and what you truly believe when you pray? It is vital to come before the Lord with openness about one's life, deeds and actions. Daniel 9:4-10 is an excellent guideline for confession of sin, both personal and national. Another vital aspect of biblical prayer is the giving of thanks to the Lord. Psalm 136 is an outline and list of that for which one can and should be thankful. All giving of thanks is based upon the mantra throughout the Psalm, "His love endures forever."

Jesus was very clear in Matthew 7:7-8 (BSB) in what is referred to as an A.S.K. acrostic: "ASK and it will be given to you; SEEK and you will find; KNOCK and the door will be opened to you. For everyone who ASKS receives; the one who SEEKS finds; and to the one who KNOCKS, the door will be opened." How often should one pray? First Thessalonians 5:18 states: "Pray without ceasing (without hesitancy; continually; persistently; never stop or give up)." Prayerfully – consider these things with me.

21. Prayer

To Remember:

Prayer is communication and fellowship
directly with the Triune God.

It means a conscious awareness of
being in His presence.

22. The Glory of God's Presence

It is very compelling when a worship service begins with the Congregation singing movingly the words written by Steven Lee Fry:

> Oh, the glory of Your presence
> We Your temple, Give You reverence.
> Come and rise from Your rest
> And be blessed by our praise
> As we glory in Your embrace,
> As Your Presence Now fills this place.

For reflection and practice, two passages of God's Word direct complete focus upon God and His Glory. First is Psalm 24:7-8, "Lift up your heads, O gates! And be lifted up, O ancient doors, that the King of glory may come in. Who is this King of glory? The Lord, strong and mighty, the Lord, mighty in battle!" Second is First Corinthians 10:31, "So, whether you eat or drink, or whatever you do, do all to the glory of God."

In the devotional: Get More Strength for The Journey, Joseph Stowell reflects on God's glory and stated:

> "God's glory is the manifestation of all that He is in His unsurpassed, stunning perfection. It is His amazing love, His wide mercy, His deep grace. His glory is seen in His truth, justice, wisdom, and power. To glorify Him means that we have the high privilege of showing Him off in a world that is totally unaware of what He is really like. Acts of mercy to the undeserving, grace to the needy, forgiveness to an offender, living wisely

according to His will - all give glorious visibility to the character and quality of our God."

This reflection should cause us to remember Westminster Shorter Catechism No.1: "The chief end of mankind is to glorify God and enjoy Him forever." It dovetails neatly with the question in Second Corinthians 6:16 where the Apostle Paul asks and answers a vital question that should impact us all: "What agreement can exist between the temple of God and idols? For we are the temple of the living God." When Solomon's Temple was completed and the Ark of the Covenant was carried into it, First Kings 8:10-11 indicates: "And when the priests came out of the holy place, a cloud filled the house of the Lord, so that the priests could not stand to minister because of the cloud, for the glory of the Lord filled the house of the Lord."

Question: If we are the temple of the Living God today, shouldn't His glory be evident in it and radiate from it? Is that happening in the lives of professing Christians today? What is our reasonable excuse if that isn't taking place? Could it mean that some are not taking a serious God seriously? A reality check: As or when people enter the church building, what do they observe? What do they sense? What is their first impression? Equally importantly, what is their second impression? Will they return? If so, why? What could one reasonably expect their second impression to be?

The ultimate question: Did the people entering the church building have an immediate awareness of the presence of God in that place? Do we truly believe and sense the words of the opening Hymn: "As Your presence now fills this place"? How do we measure God's presence in our midst? By what means do we make such an assessment? Prayerfully – Consider these things with me!

To Remember:

God is always serious about His receiving
all glory and honor – all of the time.
We should anticipate all of what it means
to be living in His presence.

23. Perfection

Perspective and Reality Moment

The biblical Christian has a high standard, challenge and goal that has been placed upon us by Jesus Christ. In the Sermon on the Mount, Jesus made this statement to His disciples and those who began following Him, Matthew 5:46-48 (ESV), "For if you love those who love you, what reward do you have? Do not even the tax collectors do the same? And if you greet only your brothers, what more are you doing than others? Do not even the gentiles do the same? You therefore must be perfect, as your heavenly Father is perfect." Here is the forceful declaration: "You must be perfect, as your heavenly Father is perfect."

How does one begin to grasp what it means to be perfect and how that perfection can be gained? A commentator (Barnes Notes) suggests: "The Savior concludes this part of the discourse by commanding his disciples to be 'perfect.' This word commonly means 'finished, complete, pure, holy.' Originally, it is applied to a piece of mechanism, as a machine that is complete in its parts. Applied to people, it refers to completeness of parts, or perfection, where no part is defective or wanting."

Second Corinthians 7:1 shares this stipulation and thought: "Since we have these promises, dear friends, let us purify ourselves from everything that contaminates body and spirit, perfecting holiness out of reverence for God." The preceding verses in Second Corinthians 6:14-18 (NIV) share a series of contrasts where definitive choices must be made. Then follows a series of promises by a covenant-keeping God. The contrasts and promises are progressively achievable goals. Just as sanctification is an ongoing process, the same is true in terms of the perfection one is to seek after.

Added to this process are the words of Hebrews 12:1-2 (NIV), "Since we are surrounded by such a great cloud of witnesses (those named in Hebrews 11), let us throw off everything that hinders and the sin that so easily entangles. And let us run with perseverance the race marked out for us, fixing our eyes on Jesus, the author and the one who perfects our faith." God is at work within His people to will and to do all of His good pleasure in us and through us (Philippians 2:13). It is reassuring to know how this process is working and what will be accomplished in due time. Will there be challenges and struggles? Yes! Will there be times when one stumbles along the way? Yes! On the narrow way, when one stumbles, will here be someone who will assist and lift one up? Yes!

There is a very dramatic reading of Isaiah 40:21-31 in the film, *Chariots of Fire*. Eric Liddell, a missionary designee to China is seen in a church reading this passage. As a film backdrop, there are those who are participants in Track Events. It is especially dramatic and memorable when he reads: verses 28-31 (NASB), "Do you not know? Have you not heard? The Everlasting God, the Lord, the Creator of the ends of the earth does not become weary or tired. His under-standing is inscrutable. He gives strength to the weary. And to him who lacks might, He increases power. Though youths grow weary and vigorous young men stumble badly, yet those who wait upon the Lord will gain new strength; they will mount up with wings like eagles, they will run and not get tired, they will walk and not faint." In viewing the film as these words were being read, there were men who stumbled badly – but – they got up, although sore and covered with dirt and mud – they got back up and finished the race.

A final word of assurance for us is Psalm 18:30, "As for God, his way is perfect: The LORD's word is flawless; he

shields all who take refuge in him." It is important to remember that God has a perfect plan for each life. The closer one is to Him, the greater will be the knowledge of His working to accomplish that plan. We should note and remember Philippians 2:13, "For it is God who works in you to will and to act on behalf of His good pleasure."
Prayerfully – consider these things with me.

To Remember:

The Eternal God always knows what is best for His people
in all circumstances and at all times.
He is always able to do much more
than one can ask or imagine.
~ Ephesians 3:20 ~

24. Bought and Owned

Perspective and Reality Moment

There is a very compelling passage of Scripture that underscores the special relationship that God wants with His people at all times. It is expressed in Isaiah 43:1-3 (ESV), "But now thus says the Lord, He who created you...He who formed you: Fear not, for I have redeemed (bought) you; I have called you by name, you are mine (personal possession). When you pass through the waters, I will be with you; and through the rivers, they shall not overwhelm you; when you walk through fire you shall not be burned, and the flame shall not consume you. For I am the Lord your God."

There is also this reminder in First Corinthians 6:20, "For you have been bought with a price: therefore, glorify God in your body." My soul was blest and conscience pricked when I read the following that someone (source unknown) posted: "Think of how wonderful it would be if someone in your world were to see a God sighting by watching your life. Think of it - each day we have a chance to give someone a God-sighting as the attitudes and character of Jesus are seen through us. And, in fact, providing God-sightings is God's intended purpose for our lives, so that all can finally believe that Jesus really lives."

In First Corinthians 6:20, we are told that Jesus paid a great price so that we might live to glorify Him. God's glory is the manifest expression of all that He is in His all-surpassing, praiseworthy, stunning perfection! And glorifying Him is quite simply showing off the reality of His glorious character in all of our actions, encounters, and attitudes. It's making the invisible God visible. And He has chosen to make His love, mercy, grace, justice, righteousness, holiness, and every other aspect of His stunning character visible through you and me!

The place where it should prick one's conscience is thinking about and contemplating the ramifications of: When was the last time you stunned your world by loving someone who is unlovable? By forgiving a deep offense caused by another? By choosing integrity over compromise? By serving others instead of serving yourself? By reaching out to the poor and oppressed? By extending grace to an undeserving soul? What a privilege! We have been bought and owned so that we may represent our Owner in a world that needs His redemption (being bought back). The last line in a Hymn Refrain (He Lives, A.H. Ackley) asks and answers a vital question and gives an equally vital response: "You ask me how I know He lives, He lives within my heart."

A special friend on Facebook, wrote: "Any ideas, whether old or new, cannot be advanced by one who suffers from amnesia; part of the past is needed in the present if it is to reach the future. Ideas need clarity to become positively contagious in order to affect others that can help carry them on! (S.L.)" To which, I responded: Sometimes – it depends on what one's past included. Sometimes – there are scars borne by those who were told they were unwanted and would never amount to anything – those who seldom heard the words that emulate the Savior's love, mercy and grace! They have traveled through life with burdens and baggage that has been a limitation to any sense of self-worth. They can be mired down by thinking they have nothing to say that others would listen no – nothing to share that others would want. That's a reason why some love the verses in Scripture that begin with – "But God…" What a difference He can and does make in one's life. All of us need to prayerfully – prepare our heart and life to be all of what Jesus wants and intends for it to be. Prayerfully – Consider these things with me!

To Remember:

Since we usually have only one opportunity
to make a good first impression for God,
we should let our light shine before men,
that they may see our good deeds and
glorify our Father in heaven.
~ Matthew 5:16 (BSB) ~

25. The Church: Waxing or Waning

Perspective and Reality Moment

Throughout the decades of my life, there has never been a time when a church was not part of it. A question that is pervasive asks: What is the church and what characterizes it? In a devotional compiled from his book, *The Set of the Sail*, Dr. A. W. Tozer shares a very concise concept of what the church is supposed to be. At the very least,

> The church is born out of the gospel and that gospel has to do with God and man's relation to God. Christianity engages to bring God into human life, to make men right with God, to give them a heart knowledge of God, to teach them to love and obey God and ultimately to restore in them the lost image of God in full and everlasting perfection.

As the parameter and guideline for The Church, he utilized First Corinthians 1:2, "To the church...to those sanctified in Christ Jesus and called to be holy, together with all those everywhere who call on the name of our Lord Jesus Christ - their Lord and ours." A thought attached is, "The church is the people of God, the family of God. Wherever the people of God are the church is. We are members of Christ's body in the world. We are not confined to a church building. We are the church wherever we are." Attached to this devotional is a prayer:

"O Lord, may Your church be the church-bold and unashamed. We are Your people through whom You seek to reach those around us."

The place where The Church begins is when a person enters into both a commitment and discipline as expressed in Psalm 27:8, "You have said, Seek my face. My heart says to you, Your face, Lord, do I seek." It will also include the words of Jesus to the Samaritan woman in John 4:23-24, "But a time is coming and has now come when the true worshipers will worship the Father in spirit and in truth, for the Father is seeking such as these to worship Him. God is a Spirit, and His worshipers must worship Him in spirit and in truth."

Over the years, I have read and experienced varying views about the church - its structure and function. There is obvious disagreement about the subject of the church manifested by the various groups in communities across this nation and world. Just as obvious is that several of them are wrong in how they determine and define the church and its rituals. Who is more correct – The Baptists or the Roman Catholics? Who dominates the world stage with "churches"? Is the Pentecostal movement more Biblical than the United Methodists, etc.? Generally, the answer would be – No!

One should appreciate the approach of Peter to the church during a dispersion period. In First Peter 1:3-6, as the Church is driven from its buildings and their antiquities destroyed due to persecution, that which defines who the people of God are is stated as:

> "Blessed be the God and Father of our Lord Jesus Christ! By His great mercy, He has given us new birth into a living hope through the resurrection of Jesus Christ from the dead, and into an inheritance that is imperishable, undefiled, and unfading, reserved in heaven for you, who through faith are protected by God's power for the salvation that is ready to be revealed in the last time. In this you greatly rejoice."

Prayerfully – consider these things with me.

To Remember:

Jesus prayed that His people
should be one just as the Triune God is one.
~ John 17 ~

How are we doing?
What does the watching world observe?
Is the Head of the Church pleased with His people?

26. Irrational Calculations

Perspective and Reality Moment

At the outset of the twenty-first century, we have come through a period of history that crystallizes for us the direction we are now heading at an increasing rate of acceleration. We can generalize and indicate that it has become the cultural norm of our day. However, that would be a misrepresentation of the propensity of the human heart, emotions and irrational calculations that are imbedded within every human being. Left unchecked and undisciplined, it will rapidly contribute to societal disarray and increasing decadence. We have fallen prey to allowing for irresponsibility while assuming we are privileged and entitled. We have seen countless numbers of public figures who give excuses for actions taken and resorting to blaming others for the prevailing conditions and trends. Few, if any, step forward and accept responsibility for an action. It's almost as though they and we are living within a vacuum.

The more the culture ignores the Eternal God and His infallible word, the more the use of excuses and the use of blame will increase. On one occasion, the Lord Jesus Christ shared a sweeping truth in The Parable of The Great Supper - Luke 14:12-24. In verses 17-18, there is a sad summary where the Master of the house has extended his invitation and the ensuing response: "Come, for all things are now ready. But they all with one accord began to make excuses." The MSG renders the text: "They all began to beg off, one after another making excuse." When an excuse is given, it is the attempt to be released from an obligation or duty. The Oxford Dictionary indicates that it is: "A reason put forward to conceal the real reason for an action; a pretext."

We find that the readiness to offer excuses and blame began shortly after Creation. When Adam and Eve succumbed to the temptation of the serpent in the Garden of Eden, it would alter their personal privilege and that of all following generations. Adam and Eve had become accustomed to the regular evening visits by God in the cool of the evening. One can only imagine how unique that fellowship must've been. The change occurred after they had disobeyed God's one command to them. They had always anticipated God coming to meet with them, but now Genesis 3:8-13 describes their behavior: "Adam and Eve heard the sound of the Lord God walking in the Garden in the cool of the day, and the man and his wife hid themselves from the presence of the Lord God among the trees in the Garden. But the Lord God called to the man and said to him: Where are you?" The obvious should be pointed out that God knew what Adam and Eve had done and also knew precisely where they were. The biblical principle that should always be remembered by us is given in Hebrews 4:13, "And no creature is hidden from His sight, but all are naked and exposed to the eyes of Him to Whom we must give account." But Adam, like us, tried to explain why he was hiding.

The Genesis 3 text continues: "Adam said: I heard the sound of You in the garden and I was afraid, because I was naked, and so I hid myself." The obvious question he and we have to answer is: "Who told you that you were naked?" Another question follows: Did you disobey Me? "Have you eaten of the tree of which I commanded you not to eat?" Now the blame game begins. "The man said (blamed): the woman whom you gave to be with me, she gave me the fruit of the tree, and I ate." The text continues: "Then the Lord God said to the woman: What is this that you have done?" She also has someone to blame: "The woman said (blamed), the serpent (you created) deceived me, and I ate." The trend is so easily repeated in every context of life: (Luke 14:18) "They all with one accord began to make excuses." The personal application pertains to how you and I respond to the Lord God. Are we any different than Adam or Eve? Do we believe our excuses will be received favorably by our God? Steve Green wrote a lyric that can serve as a prayer:

> "Oh, may all who come behind us find us faithful.
> May the fire of our devotion light their way.
> May the footprints that we leave
> lead them to believe and the lives we live
> inspire them to obey.
> Oh, may all who come behind us find us faithful."

Prayerfully - consider these things with me.

To Remember:

Don't fake it! Always be honest before the Lord your God!

27. Sanctuaries

Perspective and Reality Moment

In the daily news (2016-2017), we heard and read much about Sanctuary Cities. They were being established as part of a trend in this nation to deal with the emerging illegal or undocumented people entering the nation. Despite the Federal Law, cities and states across the nation have chosen to defy rather than to comply with the law. Overall, Sanctuary Cities are designed as safety zones for those who would otherwise be deported to their nation of origin.

Interestingly, when the children of Israel entered The Promised Land, cities of refuge were part of that inheritance. The Levites were the only tribe not to have a land designation inasmuch as they were priests of the Lord and the overseers of the Tabernacle, its rites and furnishings (Numbers 2:5-13). The Levites were to be scattered across the entire land and were to inhabit 48 cities (Numbers 35:6-7). Of those cities, 6 were designated as cities of refuge (Joshua 20:7-8).

The "Sanctuary Cities" of the Old Testament were for a much different purpose than those being set aside currently. The Mosaic Law indicated that anyone who committed a murder was to be put to death (Exodus 21:14). However, for unintentional deaths, God's Law required Cities of Refuge to which the murderer could flee (Exodus 21:13). In such a place, the murderer would be free from the avenger until the case would go to trial (Numbers 35:19). The designated peoples could judge the merits of the case and determine if the attacker acted maliciously or unintentionally. If the attacker left the place of refuge, the avenger would pursue his right to kill the murderer (Numbers 35:24-28).

There is a much different application for a "Sanctuary" that Randy Scruggs (1982) wrote as a prayer:

Lord, prepare me to be a sanctuary
Pure and holy, tried and true.
With thanksgiving, I'll be a living
Sanctuary for You.

Lead Me on Lord, from temptation
Purify me, from within.
Fill my heart with, Your Holy Spirit
Take away all my sin.

Prayerfully – consider these things with me.

To Remember:

Our hope of glory is based upon the
presence of the Triune God in our lives today.

28. When Right Side Up Is Upside Down

Perspective and Reality Moment

Prior to New Year's Eve (2009), the mood of the country was: Let's have a celebration - a party! Print more money! Let's join the hollow chorus of Happy New Year! What a year 2009 has been! Stimulus packages! Corporate takeovers! Bank failures! Home foreclosures! Ongoing wars and mounting tensions! Nuclear capability of unstable governments! Economic uncertainty! Apparent shift from capitalism to socialism! We voted for change and change we got. If it fails – blame the former President! If it succeeds – well – we'll just have to wait until that happens. The year 2010 is going to be a super year when everything is supposed to fall into place and millions of jobs are supposed to be created.

Meanwhile – since a terrorist without a passport got on an airliner with explosives in his under-shorts – now the demand is for equipment to do nude searches. That's what needs to be done – inconvenience, humiliation, delay the law-abiding citizen – but – let's not profile a terrorist from Yemen! Don't demand a passport from him! He deserves rights! Get him a lawyer! Read him his Miranda Rights! Make certain he gets returned to his native country so he can assist in the training of future terrorists. Don't put him in Gitmo (Guantanamo, Cuba) as a military combatant! That's a former President tactic! Let's not be cynical but believe in this country and its leaders!

A friend (WBL), a widower for several years, included the following in a Christmas letter when he was age 93. He wrote:

> "Today, I am thinking of a very alarming prediction in Scripture, and am praying daily for my family, and my extended family!! That we will all be

prepared well for the coming of the antichrist, and the persecution of the church, predicted in Revelation 13. So alarming!

Our world is now being prepared according to our Lord's predictions in his Olivet Discourse (Matthew 24 and 25), and elsewhere in Scripture, for the momentous days ahead! I have asked our Lord that I might live until he comes again! No assurance of this yet! But, perhaps he is allowing me to live so I can pray daily for all parents as you faithfully are bringing up your little ones in the faith, and the knowledge of God's word!

This Scripture tells us that God will allow one final, terrible war against the people of God, a world-wide struggle for the souls of men. Never believe the lie...that this man is God, no matter how amazing his miracles!! Test him by what he says about our Lord, about the Word of God, and God's way of salvation!! But, in Christ, no matter how severe the test, our triumph is assured! Satan is already a defeated foe! But some of us may be called upon to lay down our lives for our Lord!

Personally, I am now convinced that the great rebellion predicted in Second Thessalonians 2, is the world-wide rise of Islam that we are seeing today! I believe also that their Mahdi, their savior, their messiah whom they believe is coming very soon, will be one and the same with the antichrist predicted in our Bibles! President Ahmadinejad of Iran, has spent millions preparing the mosque in Qom, near Tehran, for his arrival!"

Some may shrug this off as they do most things in life! That's part of the culture and lifestyle that has become the comfort zone in this nation. Priorities are upside down! With all the unemployment and hunger around us, thousands of people will spend thousands of dollars to go to college and professional football bowl games! Some will spend what they don't have for this momentary pleasure. Edward Gibbon writing about The Decline of The Roman Empire:

> "...placed the blame on a loss of civic virtue among the Roman citizens. They gradually entrusted the role of defending the Empire to barbarian mercenaries who eventually turned on them. He considered that Christianity had contributed to this, making the populace less interested in the worldly here-and-now and more willing to wait for the rewards of heaven. The decline of Rome was the natural and inevitable effect of immoderate greatness. Prosperity ripened the principle of decay; the causes of destruction multiplied with the extent of conquest; and as soon as time or accident had removed the artificial supports, the stupendous fabric yielded to the pressure of its own weight..."

Can it happen in our nation? Is it happening before our eyes? Look! See! Comprehend! The reminder of First Thessalonians 5:6 should be always before us: "Let us not sleep, as others do, but let us keep awake and be sober." In terms of Christ coming again, Mark 13:33-34 should also be noted: "Be on guard, keep awake. For you do not know when the time will come (for His return). Prayerfully - Consider these things with me!

To Remember:

Scripture urges us to consider God's now – today.
Waiting unto later date is unacceptable and
may prove to be too little – too late.

29. If "I" Were King

The King and I is a musical by Richard Rodgers and Oscar Hammerstein II based on the book Anna and the King of Siam by Margaret Landon. The plot comes from the memoirs of Anna Leonowens, who became school teacher to the children of King Mongkut of Siam in the early 1860s. Wikipedia contains a good summary of this production: "The King is quite pleased with Anna's teaching. His eldest son Prince Chulalongkorn has some concerns, however. The young prince asks his father when he will know he knows everything and thus be ready to rule. The King gives him hope, but when he is alone, reveals that he himself is troubled; he does not know how best to rule. In the meantime, Anna tells the children that she has grown to like them. Then she launches into a new lesson - geography - having just received a more accurate map from England. The new map shows Siam in its proper size in relation to other countries. She has to end her lesson prematurely, though, when Prince Chulalongkorn refuses to believe that Siam is so small and that there is such a substance as snow. His father rescues Anna by ordering the children to believe her."

There is a death-bed scene when all of the King's children are brought to the King. "Prince Chulalongkorn is a combination of his father's self-assured leadership and his mother's careful wisdom. Prince Chulalongkorn brings to Anna's classroom a healthy skepticism and a junior version of his father's arrogance.

While the king is dying, the young prince makes his first proclamations, one of which is to abolish the established tradition of bowing low to the ground 'like a toad'; instead, he wants his people to show their respect with straight backs and a confident look in their eyes. His display of command and concern for his people demonstrate his readiness to rule as well as his successful assimilation of modern Western thought."

It is always good to remember who and where one is in terms of position and responsibility. In the world of politics, too often one is subjected to the bellicosity so typical of the politician. There can be a fixation on: "If 'I' were King..." They become fixated on "I" rather than the people who elected them. Peggy Noonan points out in her column on Friday, December 4th, 2009 regarding the President's address to the nation from West Point:

"...there was too much "I" in the speech. George H.W. Bush famously took the word "I" out of his speeches - we called them "I-ectomies" - because of a horror of appearing to be calling attention to himself. Mr. Obama is plagued with no such fears. When "I" took office..." I" approved a long-standing request...After consultations with our allies "I" then..." I" set a goal." That's all from one paragraph. Further down he used the word "I" in three paragraphs an impressive 15 times. "I" believe "I" know, "I" have signed..."I" have read..."I" have visited. I, I—ay yi yi. This is a man badly in need of an "I"-ectomy. After the President announced his plan he seemed to slip in: "After 18 months, our troops will begin to come home...Then came the reference to July 2011 as the date departure begins. It was startling to hear a compelling case for our presence followed so quickly by an abrupt announcement of our leaving. It sounded like a strategy based on the song Groucho Marx used to sing, "Hello, I must be going."

Interestingly, there is a similar biblical issue with Lucifer prior to his being cast out of heaven by God. It was his need for an "I"-ectomy. In Isaiah 14:12-15, the prophet states:

> "How you are fallen from heaven, O Day Star...How you are cut down to the ground...You who said in your heart, "I" will ascend to heaven; above the stars of God "I" will set my throne on high; "I" will sit on the mount of assembly in the far reaches of the north; "I" will ascend above the heights of the clouds; "I" will make myself like the Most High. But you are brought down to Sheol, to the far reaches of the pit."

The self-confident and self-assured should pay attention to the words of First Corinthians 10:12, "...let anyone who thinks that he stands take heed lest he fall." The Message takes some liberties with its translation but maintains the basic focus: "Don't be so naive and self-confident. You're not exempt. You could fall flat on your face as easily as anyone else. Forget about self-confidence; it's useless. Cultivate God-confidence." Prayerfully - Consider these things with me!

To Remember:

Spiritual Surgery requires that
the "I" cataract must be removed. Until then,
self will be dominant and all else will be a blur.

30. Impossibility

Perspective and Reality Moment

What does it take to make you want to quit? Criticism? A sense of failure? Difficult circumstances? Hardship? Handicap? Let's consider the truth of Philippians 4:13, "I can do all things through him (Jesus Christ) who strengthens me." When Jesus had told His disciples how difficult it would be for a person of wealth to enter the Kingdom of God, they asked (Mark 10:26-27, ESV), "Then who can be saved? Jesus looked at them and said: With man it is impossible, but not with God. For all things are possible with God." The encouragement for the people of God is that all things are possible with God – despite hardship or handicaps; despite criticism or opposition; despite unknown and untold circumstances – everything is possible with God.

A man who clearly understood this was Eugene L. Clark. He had been a staff musician with Back to the Bible Broadcast with Theodore Epp. Eugene Clark literally personified the title of his famous song, "Nothing Is Impossible." Although his fingers once flew across the piano keyboard, he later became a victim of crippling arthritis and he also became totally blind. When it finally became impossible for Clark to continue playing the organ or piano, he requested that they bring to his bedside a dictating machine. With this marvelous electric invention and his most valuable possession, a keen mind, he continued to give to the world his beautiful musical offering. A note, a rest, a bar, and a dot at a time, the machine has recorded the product of his active mind—something that neither total blindness nor crippling arthritis could conquer.

Hundreds of gospel songs and hymns, scores of choir arrangements, and three missionary cantatas have flowed through his dedicated heart and mind into the Christian world. His best-known song, "Nothing Is Impossible," was introduced in 1964. Clark was quick to credit his wife with a great deal of the success of his ministry. Her love, loyalty, and patience were invaluable assets to his work.

(1) I read in the Bible the promise of God,
That nothing for Him is too hard;
Impossible things He has promised to do,
If we faithfully trust in His Word.
Refrain:

Nothing is impossible when you put your trust in God;
Nothing is impossible when you're trusting in His Word.
Hearken to the voice of God to thee:
"Is there anything too hard for Me?"
Then put your trust in God alone and rest upon His Word--
For everything, O everything,
Yes, everything is possible with God!

(2) The word of the Lord is an anchor secure,
When winds of uncertainty blow:
Though man in his weakness may falter and fail,
His Word will not fail us we know.

(3) All things are possible, this is His Word,
Receive it 'tis written for you,
Believe in His promises, God cannot fail,
For what He has said He will do.

To Remember:

Impossibility exists and prevails for those

who stop seeking God and believing in His Power.
Seek Him and you will find Him.
Prayerfully – Consider these things with me.

31. Can A Little Child Like Me?

Perspective and Reality Moment

A public domain Children's Hymn written by Mary M. Dodge (1877) asks: "Can A Little Child Like Me, thank the Father fittingly?" The answer is: Yes! There was a moment in the ministry of Jesus when the disciples tried to prevent the little children from coming to Him. In Matthew 19:13-14 (BSB), the following scene is recorded: "The little children were brought to Jesus for Him to place His hands on them and pray for them; and the disciples rebuked those who brought them. But Jesus said: Let the little children come to Me, and do not hinder them! For the kingdom of heaven belongs to such as these."

What is interesting about this scene and the words of Jesus is that previously this was a point of discussion with the disciples when they were focused on the pecking order of who would be the greatest in the kingdom. Jesus stated clearly in Matthew 18:1-6 (BSB), answering the question of the disciples:

> "Truly I tell you, He said, unless you change and become like little children, you will never enter the kingdom of heaven. Therefore, whoever humbles himself like this little child is the greatest in the kingdom of heaven. And whoever welcomes a little child like this in My name welcomes Me. But if anyone causes one of these little ones who believe in Me to stumble, it would be better for him to have a large millstone hung around his neck and to be drowned in the depths of the sea."

A serious Savior is stating and establishing a serious kingdom principle to which the disciples should – must – adhere. Very quickly, the lesson was either ignored or forgotten and the disciples were attempting to keep the children away from Jesus. If it is that easy to personalize the simple teaching of Jesus and ignore its application, how will the deeper responsibilities, such is The Sermon on the Mount, be personally applied?

My wife and I have a Great Grandson, Keaton, who was diagnosed with Leukemia when he was 2 ½ years old. At a point, the Medical Team believed it was in remission. However, it returned with a vengeance. He is now aged 7 and is being treated and prepared for a Stem Cell Transplant. Having tried all of the regular protocols for such treatment, the Medical Team is now proceeding with a Trial Treatment. Part of the concern has been Keaton's reactions to this treatment. He had become non-responsive for four continuous days. At this point of time, we have no hint of whether or not this Trial Treatment will prove to be successful. Some of this need was posted as a Prayer Request in different Facebook formats. Several responses were received. Two of them, used by permission, are:

> "James Perry's great grandson Keaton Barron has taught me a lot about grace and love. I just had a conversation with my neighbor who loves the OKC Thunder and hates Kevin Durant. I told him about Keaton's battle with cancer and how Kevin Durant supported him in his first battle and is still praying for Keaton. When KD came back to OKC for the first time this past season, he was overwhelmingly rejected. Keaton was at the game with a sign welcoming KD back to OKC. My neighbor just saw the love of Jesus in Keaton's life. I pray it continues to transform my neighbor's life. He said "I am not a religious guy but I

will pray for Keaton, he has caused me to rethink what it means to love others." I invited he and his wife over for dinner."

I shared this note with our family and a few caring friends and wrote: "Rejoice in the Lord with us." One of those caring friends is a young woman, mother of four children (one of whom is autistic), and whose husband is currently being treated for Colon Cancer. She has been Institutionalized at least twice for treatment. Her situation is one of deep depression. She has done magnificently well and is an ongoing inspiration to several. The joy of the Lord exudes from her. She also posts some of the more encouraging spiritual graphics. After receiving the above note, she immediately responded:

> "Wow! God never ceases to amaze me! He can and will be ever present in the most trying of times. That story sure stirred up my soul with Joy! I love how He's working through little Keaton's life. Will continue fervently praying for him. He is loved by so many!"

When I was a child, my siblings and I attended a small group that was once a rescue mission type ministry. Whenever they had a Communion Service, part of their established ritual was the reading and recitation of First Corinthians 13 and Romans 12. In Romans 12:15 (BSB), there is a very clear statement that some find difficult to apply: "Rejoice with those who rejoice; weep with those who weep."

Admittedly, we live in stressful and difficult times. Many people are overwhelmed with their personal challenges in life. There are days when one does not know what to do or how to cope with the circumstances in which they find themselves. Some of the Scripture verses that serve as a reminder for me and my focus upon others are: First Samuel 12:23 (NIV), "As for me, far be it from me that I should sin against the LORD by failing to pray for you." Galatians 6:2 (NIV), "Carry each other's burdens, and in this way, you will fulfill the law of Christ." Isaiah 53:4 (ESV), "Surely, he has borne our griefs and carried our sorrows." additional verses that should serve as an anchor for each of us and our varying needs, situations and circumstances is:

Isaiah 41:9-10 (NLT), "I have chosen you and will not throw you away. Don't be afraid, for I am with you. Don't be discouraged, for I am your God. I will strengthen you and help you. I will hold you up with my victorious right hand."

The words of older Hymns are inspiring and challenging. One of them was written by John H. Yates in 1891. One stanza expresses:

His banner over us is love,
our sword the Word of God.
We tread the road the saints above,
with shouts of triumph trod.
By faith, they like a whirlwind's breath,
swept on o'er every field.
The faith by which they conquered death
Is still our shining shield.

Refrain:
Faith is the victory! Faith is the victory!
O glorious victory, that overcomes the world.

The One Who assures our victory is our God, our strength, our refuge, our fortress, The One in Whom we can trust. Prayerfully – Consider these things with me.

To Remember:

Always trust in the Lord with all your heart and

31. Can A Litttle Child Like Me?

never lean to your own understanding or solutions. (Proverbs 3:5-6)

32. Persecution Perspicacity

Perspective and Reality Moment

Jesus Christ made it clear that the reality of persecution would befall any of His followers at any time. His words implied that it was not a matter of "if" persecution came but "when" it would occur. His concern dealt with how His disciples would respond to any stage of persecution or verbal rejection that came their way. The idea of perspicacity (the quality of having a ready insight into things; shrewdness) was to the end that His followers would develop and display "keenness of mental perception and understanding." His concern was and continues to be how one would act or react when persecution occurs.

In 1967, J.A. Peterson wrote a booklet: *Who Runs Your Life?* In 1983, it was re-published with a different title: *Your Reactions Are Showing.* Peterson was a marriage and family counselor. His motivation in writing this brief booklet was: "To help one improve his/her relationships with others and gain control of one's life by learning how to react properly and biblically." Part of his thesis was intended to crystallize the rational and ensuing actions by an individual who felt betrayed, insulted, falsely accused, arbitrarily abused, or verbally demeaned:

> "The person who reacts with anger and bitterness is being controlled by the person who offended him. How often do we let people control us in our daily life? You may be surprised to learn that your reactions to the situations you face daily may say a great deal more about you than your actions say."

The last Beatitude stated by Jesus Christ in Matthew 5 incorporates many of the negative conclusions or feelings one may have. How should one respond to these conclusions or feelings? Is the response Biblically based or retaliatory in nature? Matthew 5:10-12 (ESV), Jesus said:

> Blessed are those who are persecuted for righteousness' sake, for theirs is the kingdom of heaven.
> Blessed are you when others revile you and persecute you and utter all kinds of evil against you falsely on my account.
> Rejoice and be glad, for your reward is great in heaven, for so they persecuted the prophets who were before you.

That which Jesus Christ is requiring is one of the more difficult things to do. There is an innate desire to retaliate and to get even. An old psychological saying suggests putting the frustration where it belongs. Why should the innocent party have to deal with the consequences of the negative person for whom it matters little if he destroys a reputation or good name of another person? The Apostle Peter, who in his younger days was no slouch when it came to reacting negatively and aggressively, wrote in his epistle (First Peter 3:9 – NLT), "Don't repay evil for evil. Don't retaliate with insults when people insult you. Instead, pay them back with a blessing." That is what God has called you to do, and he will bless you for it.

An example of this type response is given in Second Samuel 16:5-14 (ESV). Absalom has usurped the throne and made himself King. As David journeys away from Jerusalem, "a man from the house of Saul named Shimei came and cursed David continually." He called David "a man of blood" and "a worthless man." One of David's mighty men wanted to confront Shimei and take off his head. But David insisted on restraint with these words: "Leave him alone and let him curse…It may be that the Lord will repay me with good for his cursing today." In addition to his cursing, Shimei was also throwing physical stones and dust at David.

How would you have reacted if someone was throwing stones, mud and dust at you? How would you respond if someone was cursing you and making accusations against you? How would Jesus Christ want you to act or react? Luke 6:23 (ESV) records: "Rejoice in that day, and leap for joy, for behold, your reward is great in heaven." Prayerfully – consider these things with me.

To Remember:

Not I, but Christ, be honored, loved, exalted;
Not I, but Christ, be seen be known, be heard;
Not I, but Christ, in every look and action,
Not I, but Christ, in every thought and word.
~ A.B. Simpson ~

33. Tranquility or Turbulence

Perspective and Reality Moment

Most of us desire and want tranquility rather than turbulence. We trend towards peace and quiet rather than turmoil and noise. All of us have a built-in decibel level beyond which our comfort zones cannot stretch or go. Entering into this mix in our generation is terrorism where tranquility is not part of their ambition or core value. Terrorism is suggested to have a narrow objective: "Their goal isn't necessarily to bring down the United States government, just to batter it so much that it accedes to the attackers' will." Its intention is not so much to occupy as it is to disrupt. Turbulence serves them as an ally and is part of their foundational principles.

Most of us would associate turbulence with air currents violently vibrating an aircraft. There are also storms at sea and the tossing of vessels of all sizes. We experience turbulence with weather patterns that shift and produce storms and wind advisories. Some of the definitions for turbulence is: "violent disorder or commotion; a state of violent disturbance and disorder; instability in the atmosphere; a disturbed state; tumult; disorder; agitation…"

In a column by Peggy Noonan in the Wall Street Journal (November 2008), her comments were titled: "Turbulence Ahead - Some things to be thankful for in depressing times." In the article, she draws a distinction between the great depression that occurred in the 1930s with the events that are occurring in 2008. She concluded that the economic downturn is dissimilar to the great depression and uses statistics and impressions to make her point. There is a word that would help her article, namely, "yet"! We are not in a Great

Depression II – yet! However – don't tell that to the people where foreclosure is occurring with their homes; or the household provider who has been told his employment is no longer available; or the number of businesses that are closing; or the number of people who cannot pay a minimum amount on their bills; or the fixed-income citizens whose annuity-pension has almost disappeared. We are not at a great depression level – yet!

Consider these things: The Bible contains some important references and perspectives to this entire subject of turbulence versus tranquility. First, Isaiah 57:20-21, "But the wicked are like the troubled sea, when it cannot rest, whose waters cast up mire and dirt. There is no peace, Says my God, for the wicked." This assessment/judgment pertains to those in Verse 17, "For the iniquity of his covetousness I was angry and struck him; I hid and was angry, And, he went on backsliding in the way of his heart." Second, John 14:27, "Peace I leave with you, My peace I give to you; not as the world gives do I give to you. Let not your heart be troubled, neither let it be afraid." These words are intended to encourage those who must go forward without the physical presence of Jesus Christ with them. Third, John 16:33, "These things I have spoken to you, that in Me you may have peace. In the world, you will have tribulation; but be of good cheer, I have overcome the world." Living in a troubled and tempestuous time does not mean one has to surrender to turbulence. Tranquility is being in a relationship with Jesus Christ, not with the accommodations granted by a culture/society. The Yale Divinity School (November 2007) embarked on a reconciliation mission, which states as part of its purpose:

> "The goal is to promote reconciliation between Muslims and Christians, and between Muslim nations and the West, drawing on the resources of the Abrahamic faiths and the teachings and person of

Jesus...In its initial phase, the reconciliation program is focused primarily on bridge-building scholarly research on the major theological, political, cultural, social and ethical issues which traditionally divide Muslims and Christians, and on concerns which unite them."

It will be interesting to see if/when the study will bring them to Second Corinthians 5:16 through 21, and to embrace the truth of Verses 18-19, "Now all things are of God, who has reconciled us to Himself through Jesus Christ, and has given us the ministry of reconciliation, that is, that God was in Christ reconciling the world to Himself, not imputing their trespasses to them, and has committed to us the word of reconciliation."

Too often there is laissez-faire (letting things take their own course, without interfering) approach embraced by an enlarging group of cultural citizens. This has also crept into the Church where fewer are willing to make a commitment to participate in ministry and missional efforts. There is a contentment with letting someone else do it rather than being one who is engaged and seeking to bring about a positive response. You are probably aware of the story:

There were four people named Everybody, Somebody, Anybody, and Nobody. There was an important job to be done and Everybody was sure that Somebody would do it. Anybody could have done it, but Nobody did it. Somebody got angry about that because it was Everybody's job. Everybody thought that Anybody could do it, but Nobody realized that Everybody wouldn't do it. It ended up that Everybody blamed Somebody when Nobody did what Anybody could have done.

This is too often the case when personal commitment is not present. It also allows for turbulence being endured while tranquility is sacrificed. Where do you fit into this scenario and scheme of things? Prayerfully – consider these things with me.

To Remember:

Let the Peace from God
be the foundation of your Peace with God.
~ Philippians 4 ~

34. Something Old - Something New

Perspective and Reality Moment

An old tradition is quoted by many when a bride is about to be married: "Something old, something new; something borrowed, something blue, and a silver sixpence in her shoe." The idea is that this combination as part of the bride's attire (wardrobe) will assure happiness, success, and good luck in her marriage.

The history of this tradition states: "Each item in this poem represents a good-luck token for the bride. If she carries all of them on her wedding day, her marriage will be happy. "Something old" symbolizes continuity with the bride's family and the past. "Something new" means optimism and hope for the bride's new life ahead. "Something borrowed" is usually an item from a happily married friend or family member, whose good fortune in marriage is supposed to carry over to the new bride. The borrowed item also reminds the bride that she can depend on her friends and family...In ancient Rome, brides wore blue to symbolize love, modesty, and fidelity...Before the late 19th century, blue was a popular color for wedding gowns...a silver sixpence in the bride's shoe represents wealth and financial security...For optimum fortune, the sixpence should be in the left shoe...In modern times, a dime or a copper penny is sometimes substituted..."

In political current events of 2008, it was found that there was "something old" (McCain, aged 72 [R] and Biden, aged 66 [D] – both with years in the US Senate and "something new" (Obama, aged 46 [D] and Palin, aged 44 [R] both with relatively little executive and administrative background). This is "Balancing A Ticket" run amuck (in or into a jumbled or confused state). Most of those entrenched in government certainly know the meaning of "something borrowed" inasmuch as uncontrolled spending has this nation with huge deficits. It is borrowing against the future! The idea of "something blue" doesn't apply because the appropriate color – based on the financial condition of the nation is "red"! One interesting thought that comes from the political ambition of some aspirants for office is their desire to increase the tax rate for the "rich" and to give tax relief to the "poor"! One never hears the political aspirant's acknowledgement that nearly one-third of our population (over 100 million people) pay no taxes at all. An analyst stated it this way: "...the bottom 50% of income earners in this country pay only about 3% of all individual income taxes collected by the federal government. When you get to the bottom 40% that percentage figure drops to zero..."

The greater concern is for the individual. God created a human being with a body, soul and spirit; and with a mind, emotions and a will. The "something old" is the fact of original sin – "all have sinned and have fallen short of the glory of God" (Romans 3). The possibility for "something new" is "except a man/woman be born again, he/she cannot enter the Kingdom of God" (John 3). Once this spiritual resolve is reached, the challenge and opportunity for an individual is summed up in these words: "walk in newness of life..." (Romans 6). In Galatians 5:1 [MSG]: "Christ has set us free to live a free life. So, take your stand! Never again let anyone put a harness of slavery on you." More than 50 years ago, a popular Christian camp chorus was: "Get the new look, from the old book; get the new look from the Bible...The inward look, the outward look, the upward look, from the old, old book; get the new look...from God's Word!" What should a biblical Christian believe and practice? There is an important "change" that should be sought and pursued.

34. Something Old - Something New

To Remember:

"Something old" - "let us lay aside every weight,
and the sin that so easily holds us back." (Hebrews 12:1);
"Something new" - "let us run with patience the race
set before us; looking unto Jesus…" (Hebrews 12:2).

Prayerfully – consider these things with me.

35. Jocularity

Perspective and Reality Moment

The idea of jocularity is understood by an accepted definition: "Characterized by joking; Given to joking." Humor is part of our total being. We have an emotional range that enables us to move from weeping to laughter depending on the circumstances. And indeed, the Bible allows for this range of emotion. Ecclesiastes 3:1-4 (NIV) states some obvious contrasts in life:

> "For everything there is a season, and a time for every matter under heaven: a time to be born, and a time to die; a time to plant, and a time to pluck up what is planted; a time to kill, and a time to heal; a time to break down, and a time to build up; a time to weep, and a time to laugh; a time to mourn, and a time to dance..."

The thought behind this is to realize the balance between the range of emotions and experiences so one's actions fall within the perspective of the most suitable "time" for such an expression.

When one enters into a church setting, there needs to be an understanding and refinement of what separates one thing from another. For instance, there is often some confusion regarding joy on the one hand with happiness on the other. In pausing to reflect on the possibilities, one can readily determine that much of what we intend by "happiness" is dependent on the experiences and circumstances of the moment. If one receives an unexpected gift, it results in happiness; if one expects a gift – but doesn't receive one –

then it results in unhappiness. A simple way for a church-oriented person to understand this is basically – happiness usually comes as a result of one's experience/circumstance, whereas joy always comes as a result of one's relationship with Jesus Christ. In John 15:1-11 (NIV), Jesus gives as clear a statement about this relationship when He summarizes in verse 11: "These things I have spoken to you, that my joy may be in you, and that your joy may be full."

In Ephesians 5:3 through 7, the apostle Paul establishes parameters and guidelines for the life of a follower of Jesus Christ. He couches it in terms of what is "fitting for saints" and then, states there should be "neither filthiness, nor foolish talking, nor coarse jesting, which are not fitting, but rather giving of thanks." In understanding and applying the Bible, it needs to be done with a gracious spirit. There are any number of people where one would come to the conclusion that if they ever smiled in church their face might crack! By the same token, there are those who feel jokes and humor will hold the attention of the people and develop rapport. There needs to be great care exercised to remember one is coming to a church – not a comedy club. We need to give people credit for their basic desire to gather with God's people to worship God – not to be entertained by men or musicians.

When people come to Church, they should find it as a place where there is: (1) Reverence – we are coming to Worship the Holy God; (2) Prayer – we are to enter His gates with thanksgiving, and His courts with praise; (3) Singing – psalms, hymns, spiritual songs that focus upon the Holy and sovereign God and His grace, mercy and truth; (4) Fellowship – we have come to commune with God and to focus upon Him with those of like precious faith; (5) Instruction – we need to hear God's Word accurately proclaimed so we can be exposed to "the whole counsel of God and can sense the Holy Spirit guiding us into more of God's truth and wonderful plan for our lives. We don't need artificial distractions! We don't need an effort to make us feel good! We don't need snacks and informality! We get that all week long in the places we frequent. The church is sometimes referred to as being "The Sanctuary" – a holy, sacred place of refuge and quiet. The book of Psalms is a model for us to be always focused upon the living God.

As we consider these things, let us study and put forth the sincere effort to implement Hebrews 10:23 through 25, "Let us hold fast the confession of our hope without wavering, for he who promised is faithful. And let us consider how to stir up one another to love and good works, not neglecting to meet together, as is the habit of some, but encouraging one another, and all the more as you see The Day drawing near…"

The "let us" phrases are hortatory subjunctives. A hortatory subjunctive is used in the present tense to express an exhortation or a command. Being grammatically stated "let us" does not infer it is optional but a command or exhortation to be acted upon immediately. The Book of Hebrews makes use of the hortatory subjunctive throughout the entire book. Places where the phrase is utilized: Hebrews 4:1,11,14,16. A grouping of them is in Hebrews 10:19-25. The purpose is to have one focus on the priorities of Christian living, as well as the necessity for corporate gathering to edify one another and building each other up. Prayerfully – Consider these things with me.

To Remember:

Psalm 95:1-2 (ESV)
Oh come, let us sing to the Lord;
let us make a joyful noise to the rock of our salvation!
Let us come into his presence with thanksgiving;
let us make a joyful noise to him with songs of praise!

36. Communication

Perspective and Reality Moment

A dear church officer was accustomed to remind his fellow officers: "If there's one thing that we lack around here, it's communication." Communicating accurately is not always as simple and easy as one would hope. So many factors enter into verbal communication - tone, nuance, inflection, definition, body language, etc. One needs to be guarded lest assumption of what is meant overrides what was intended by the words spoken. It's always wise to ask for clarification rather than to assume. Basic communication is, and entails (dictionary.com): "The exchange of thoughts, messages, or information, as by speech, signals, writing, or behavior. Interpersonal rapport. The art and technique of using words effectively to impart information or ideas."

For many years, a religious organization has worked to translate the Bible into every language. It was many years ago that Wycliffe Bible Translators believed there were only "2,000 tongues to go" and their literature so indicated. The more they worked with peoples all over the world, the more they began to find many tribes and dialects/sounds that were unknown to them – and so the work goes on. The Peacemaker Ministry published (08-01-08): "According to the website www.ethnologue.com, there are 6,912 living languages in the world. An interesting fact is that "347 (or approximately 5%) of the world's languages have at least one million speakers and account for 94% of the world's population. By contrast, the remaining 95% of languages are spoken by only 6% of the world's people." I also found it intriguing to learn that Papua, New Guinea has the most linguistic diversity of any country in the world--they have 820 living languages, and if you were to pick two people at random, there is a 99% chance that they would speak different languages..."

How well do we communicate with each other in an interpersonal relationship? When we read something, do we try to discern what might be in the author's mind or do we critique it based upon a personal position that has been formulated (and since "I" devised it - it must be correct and the standard by which all else is measured)? In a religious setting, an appeal can often be made to one's Hermeneutic (methodology of interpreting a Biblical text). But even there, whose Hermeneutic – Milton Terry (Classic); Bernard Ramm (Modern); or Robertson McQuilkin (Recent)? While there should be total agreement, there are different approaches to the understanding of language and interpreting an author's language. For instance, Terry states:

"Hermeneutics is the science of interpretation. The word is usually applied to the explanation of written documents, and may therefore be more specifically defined as the science of interpreting an author's language. This science assumes that there are diverse modes of thought and ambiguities of expression among men, and, accordingly, it aims to remove the supposable differences between a writer and his readers, so that the meaning of the one may be truly and accurately apprehended by the others."

Bernard Ramm's approach had variations with the classic view. It was observed about Ramm:

"In some respects Ramm's emphasis on the inner witness of the Spirit reflected the view of John Calvin, but it also reflected the influence of Karl Barth under whom he studied in Switzerland."

Ramm also had struggles with flood geology and the age of the earth. It would be easy to suggest that his hermeneutic was more subjective than objective.

There are some interesting thoughts in the Epistle of James. He enjoins that we be "slow to speak" – be accurate (1:19); "speak carefully" (2:12); and "do not speak negatively" (4:11). One's task is to communicate, wisely, clearly, factually so that another individual will be able to discern the intention and the ramification of what has been communicated. Communication seeks to pass along information and/or instruction to gain a positive response that will be demonstrated by an action that ensues.

The apostle Paul gave Timothy a word of instruction and admonition – I Timothy 4:12-16 (BSB),

> "Let no one despise your youth, but set an example for the believers in speech, in conduct, in love, in faith, in purity.
>
> Devote yourself to the public reading of Scripture, to exhortation, and to teaching.
>
> Do not neglect the gift that is in you, which was given you through the prophecy spoken over you at the laying on of the hands of the elders.
>
> Be diligent in these matters and absorbed in them, so that your progress will be evident to all.
>
> Pay close attention to your life and to your teaching.
>
> Persevere in these things, for by so doing you will save both yourself and those who hear you."

We should be defined by these words and behave like those in Malachi 3:16, "Then those who feared the Lord talked with each other, and the Lord listened and heard. A scroll of remembrance was written in his presence concerning those who feared the Lord and honored his name."

To Remember:

The watching world needs to see
your love for one another;
because it will demonstrate
to the world that you are Christ's disciples.
~ John 13 ~

37. Not Yet

Perspective and Reality Moment

When travelling as a family, the children would often ask: Are we there yet? To which, the response was often: "not yet"! On one trip, we erred when the children raised their question and the response given was: "After we get something to eat." It caused the children to express their hunger and wanting to stop and eat. For them, it meant that we would soon be near our destination. We had to quickly shift back to our former response: "Not yet"!

"Yet" is a word that is elastic in its meaning. It is used to suggest: "in the time still remaining." In a Christian context, it has been used when stating: "Be patient with me, God isn't done with me yet." We are part of a culture that desires immediacy. The level of patience can be very limited in some situations for some people. There is a purposeful concept in Psalm 37:7 (NLT) that directs one to: "Be still in the presence of the Lord, and wait patiently for him to act." In the ESV translation: "Be still before the Lord and wait patiently for him." The context of the Psalm begins with repeated use of the phrase "fret not" and instructs one to set aside worry and anxiety. Psalm 37:4-5 states that one should delight in the Lord, and to commit and trust in the Lord. The idea is to focus on the positive relationship with the Lord rather than on the negative situations and circumstances of everyday life.

Some of the negative situations and circumstances pertain to the physical and mental issues more and more people find intrusive in their lives. One of the physical issues that intrudes and overwhelms is cancer. This is one of the more insidious maladies. It begins suddenly and with little initial warning and proceeds in a gradual, subtle way with increasingly harmful effects. Despite the best medical care and treatment, which can be prolonged and costly, there is seldom a claim of one being "cured" but only that one is "in remission." It is in this regard that the word "yet" is meaningful and encouraging. In a note written to some with concern about a young child, it is a good reminder for all who have faith in God to conclude: The Great Physician is not done with this child "yet"!

With the mental issues, depression overwhelms a greater number of people dealing with the pressures and responsibilities of normal life experiences. The subtlety of it is that it can cause mood swings with an individual that can result in low self-esteem, a loss of interest in activities that are normally enjoyable, a low energy level and sometimes, a sense of pain without a clear cause. Most cases of depression are treated with medications. This can offer temporary relief but a long-term cure can be evasive and something one can only hope will become a remedy for them. They have to adjust their lives to the "not yet" in terms of a hoped-for cure.

An area where practical Christianity can be a physical and mental pressure is given in Mark 4:18-19 (BSB) - The parable of the seeds and sower. Jesus Christ explained: "Still others are like the seeds sown among the thorns. They hear the word, but the cares of this life, the deceitfulness of wealth, and the desire for other things come in and choke the word, and it becomes unfruitful. The cares of this life over-riding God's promise of provision and sustaining grace. Sadly, wrong choices and priorities can complicate one's life and frustrate the aspirations one may have. "yet" God continues to show His love, mercy, grace and care for His own. Prayerfully – Consider these things with me.

To Remember:

WHEN SATAN ASSAILS US TO STOP UP OUR PATH,
AND COURAGE ALL FAILS US,

WE TRIUMPH BY FAITH.
HE CANNOT TAKE FROM US,
THOUGH OFT HE HAS TRIED,
THIS HEART-CHEERING PROMISE,
"THE LORD WILL PROVIDE."
~ John Newton ~

38. Gloating

Perspective and Reality Moment

At times, we have all had to struggle with an inner urge to gloat over about someone or some matter. When a person has been arrogant towards another and then miscues, it would be so easy to gloat because that one has performed in an otiose (ineffective or futile; superfluous or useless) manner. Gloating is: "a feeling of great, often malicious, pleasure or self-satisfaction." We attribute such moments to our "human nature" which, if left unchecked, can be very harsh or cruel in response to another's floundering. The older generation can remember a phrase: "That one will get his comeuppance (a punishment or retribution that one deserves; one's just desert) someday." When that day eventually arrived, it allowed for a time of gloating over another's misfortune or difficulty.

There's no question about our world being in the midst of a major correction and transition. The economics are just a part of the whole. There are the advocates of global warming who ignore the natural cycles through which the world passes on a regular basis. The area of politics has received considerable notice and a considerable amount of ridicule. When one major party makes such a sweeping indictment against the other major party by campaigning against "the culture of corruption" only to face the reality that some members of their own political party are a real part of the very "culture" that was part of their campaign talking points – it is in juxtaposition to what was espoused and desired. When a political figure is targeted by a federal prosecutor and the evidence mounts that there is corruption that must be exposed, the natural tendency is to gloat, opine, and conclude – "there's another one that is getting his comeuppance." Some would even allow, it is a case of "be sure your sins will find you out." When automobile manufacturers are reprimanded in public for their mismanagement, it is too easy for one to gain satisfaction over the turmoil in an industry, as well as in individual lives. Once again, the gloat factor becomes a reality.

In biblical history (Second Samuel 16), Absalom has decided to be king and to overthrow his father, King David. As David flees Jerusalem, he is met by a man who loathes him and who sets out to ridicule and gloat over him. We note in Second Samuel 16:5-14 (NIV),

> "As King David approached…a man from the same clan as Saul's family came out from there. His name was Shimei…and he cursed as he came out. He pelted David and all the king's officials with stones, though all the troops and the special guard were on David's right and left. As he cursed, Shimei said: Get out, get out, you man of blood, you scoundrel! The Lord has repaid you for all the blood you shed in the household of Saul, in whose place you have reigned. The Lord has handed the kingdom over to your son Absalom. You have come to ruin because you are a man of blood! Then Abishai…said to the king: Why should this dead dog curse my lord the king? Let me go over and cut off his head. But the king said: What do you and I have in common, you sons of Zeruiah? If he is cursing because the Lord said to him, curse David, who can ask: why do you do this? David then said to Abishai and all his officials: My son, who is of my own flesh, is trying to take my life. How much more, then, this Benjamite! Leave him alone; let him curse, for the Lord has told him to. It may be that the Lord will see my distress and repay me with good for the cursing I am receiving today. So, David and his men continued along the road while Shimei was going

along the hillside opposite him, cursing as he went and throwing stones at him and showering him with dirt. The king and all the people with him arrived at their destination exhausted. And there he refreshed himself."

The attitude and perspective of King David is outstanding. He is the one who penned the words of Psalm 23, "…even though I walk through the valley of the shadow of death, I will fear no evil, for You are with me…" He is now in a situation where he must put these words into practice. He cannot allow himself to follow a carnal instinct and silence this voice of mockery and scorn. David has to rest in and share with others what it means to embrace: "Because the Lord is my shepherd, I have everything that I need."

When ridicule and gloating is at its zenith and is most severe, it is time to put into practice the fact of our Savior – Emmanuel – God is with us. He cannot fail and He will never leave us or forsake us. Political bluffing and/or bloviating are what they are – exaggerations and empty words. Living in the reality of Emmanuel, becomes very practical as one lives a life in the presence of God, as well as knowing the presence of the Lord wherever one goes. Emmanuel – God is with us! Prayerfully – consider these things with me.

To Remember:

Fear not, for I have redeemed you;
I have called you by name, you are mine.
When you pass through the waters, I will be with you;
and through the rivers, they shall not overwhelm you;
when you walk through fire you shall not be burned,
and the flame shall not consume you.
For I am the Lord your God.
~ Isaiah 41 ~

39. New Beginning

Perspective and Reality Moment

Words such as failure and disqualified have a heart-piercing affect upon one. The other side to this is the thought – is all failure and disqualification final? Is there any possibility of one having hope of being reinstated and/or having a second chance? Businesses on occasion file for bankruptcy and seek for time to reorganize. Many companies have come out of bankruptcy and were viable once again. Can a person who tried and failed have hope of being reorganized and becoming useful and profitable once again? Can one who was counsel to the President of the United States and who was sentenced to prison for a crime committed be recovered and restored to a constructive and useful life and ministry? Can one who tried to minister and failed be relegated to oblivion or can he be recovered and granted a new beginning for constructive and vital ministry once again?

In a Breakpoint Devotional, Chuck Colson wrote about "Admission of Failure" with a sub-title "Corrections In Crisis":

> "After serving seven months for my role in the Watergate scandal, I walked out of prison a free man. Not entirely free however, because I just could not get out of my mind the men I had met in prison - the hundreds of thousands like them in prisons across the country. So, in 1977...I started Prison Fellowship. Little could I have imagined back then that Prison Fellowship would one day be the largest Christian outreach to prisoners in the world...."

Chuck Colson pondered further:

"Why was the United States a virtual petri dish (shallow dish used for the culture of microorganisms) for growing criminals? It was not until I read the landmark 1977 study called The Criminal Personality that I was able to begin to fully appreciate what was going on. The study's authors... rebutted the conventional wisdom that crime was caused by environment-like poverty and racism. It was caused, they said, not by that, but by individuals making wrong moral choices. So, the solution to crime, they said, was "the conversion of the wrongdoer to a more responsible lifestyle." Then it hit me. Our entire penal system was seeking an institutional solution to a moral problem..." Most are aware that Prison Fellowship has had an effective ministry in providing a message of hope for the hopeless and seeing failures become successes by the grace of God.

In First Corinthians 9:24-27, the Apostle Paul wrote: "Remember that in a race everyone runs, but only one person gets the prize. You also must run in such a way that you will win. All athletes practice strict self-control. They do it to win a prize that will fade away, but we do it for an eternal prize. So, I run straight to the goal with purpose in every step. I am not like a boxer who misses his punches. I discipline my body like an athlete, training it to do what it should. Otherwise, I fear that after preaching to others I myself might be disqualified."

Disqualified is such a harsh and painful word. I can still visualize our son in High School swimming competition trying hard to win – but – he had trouble with the turns in the pool. The judge's whistle blew and a finger was pointed and the sound heard was "DQ" – disqualified. But that was one event in many! Were there other whistles, finger pointed and the "DQ" heard? Yes! But with renewed effort, there came the day when the whistle was not blown, and the finger was not pointed, and the "DQ" was not heard. Instead, he and three other swimmers had set the relay team record – a record that stood for many years in Colorado Springs.

What if at the first "DQ" our son was removed from the swim team? What if he had never been given another opportunity to try again? What if there had been condemnation for his failure and disqualification? What if there had been no second chance? What if people only remembered his failures and critiqued him on his past effort? What if he had been denied a new beginning? But – the coach worked with him and his failure became a success. Isn't that what we should do with one another – not magnify failure – but – give ourselves to help one get a new beginning – moving from failure to success?

We need to assume the role of being a Barnabas, an encourager, and join with other willing participants who will make a sincere and genuine effort to help others regain their footing with a new beginning as they move from failure to success. By doing this, we will be pleasing our Lord and Master. Prayerfully – Consider these things with me.

To Remember:

Take up thy cross, the Savior said,
if thou wouldst My disciple be;
deny thyself, the world forsake,
and humbly follow after Me.

Take up thy cross, let not its weight
fill thy weak spirit with alarm;
His strength shall bear thy spirit up,
and brace thy heart and nerve thine arm.
~ Charles W. Everest ~

40. Life Expectancy

Perspective and Reality Moment

In reading the featured stories on the World Magazine website, one of them was: "A Generous Giant - Michael Cromartie, 1950-2017." He was a man of vision and accomplishment despite the fact that few who read this knew anything about him. He died of Cancer on August 28, 2017. In his lifetime, he was able to influence some trends and individuals. In reading the article, one could learn about: (1) His certainty: "It will be glorious to meet my Savior." (2) His regret: "But for crying out loud, there's so much work I still have to do."

It reminded me of a beautiful poem by C.T. Studd, a Missionary to China, India and Africa in the 1800s that contains a recurring statement in each stanza:

> Only one life, 'twill soon be past,
> only what's done for Christ will last.

In Chapter 37 – Not Yet, a statement was made about the insidiousness of cancer and the reality that it can and does have as it unexpectedly impacts a person, families, associates and friends. We pray, encourage and assist one another as best we can and with resources available to us but we are unable to calculate the unending and expensive treatment costs. A family member who is an RN and one who has assisted in providing hospital care for cancer patients shared that one IV (intravenously administered) in the treatment plan for a child of interest costs $8,000.00 per IV. How easily and quickly the costs mount up adding to the burden of those whose loved one is being treated.

Some scripture that has come to mind (and has been shared previously), is worthy of being repeated. In a passage that's dealing with someone overtaken by/in transgression, there is an instruction that has a broader application and serves as a basic principle, Galatians 6:2-3 (NLT), "Share each other's burdens, and in this way, obey the law of Christ. If you think you are too important to help someone, you are only fooling yourself." It is directing one to be as involved as possible in the betterment and well-being of others in the varying types and stages of need. Romans 12:15-16 (ESV) states a foundational principle for one's life and practice: "Rejoice with those who rejoice, weep with those who weep." Many tears have been shed and prayers offered by various individuals for loved ones and acquaintances afflicted with cancer. Does this make a difference? Does it matter to anyone? It can and should as focus is kept upon the great physician – Jesus Christ.

Psalm 56 is about David's plight when the Philistines had captured him in Gath. Verses 1 through 12 disclose a heartfelt prayer of David to God for his uncertainty and oppression. He prays: (Verse 1-4), "Be gracious to me, O God, for man tramples on me; all day long an attacker oppresses me (they twist my words; my enemies trample on me all day long, for many attack me proudly. When I am afraid, I put my trust in you. In God, whose word I praise, in God I trust; I shall not be afraid."

A very meaningful word picture is drawn in verse 8: "You have kept count of my tossing (wandering); put my tears in your bottle. Are they not in your book?" The idea of the Lord observing how one is being oppressed; what is being said negatively about a person; and the tears that are shed before the Lord all placed carefully in God's bottle. An old hymn asks and answers: Does Jesus Care? It was written by (Frank E. Graeff, 1901). The first stanza and refrain is:

40. Life Expectancy

Does Jesus care when my heart is pained
too deeply for mirth or song,
as the burdens press, and the cares distress
and the way grows weary and long?

Refrain
Oh yes, He cares, I know He cares,
His heart is touched with my grief;
when the days are weary, the long nights dreary,
I know my Savior cares.

The abiding fact is that the eternal God is always aware
and always cares. He will accomplish His perfect will in His
perfect time. Trust in Him. He knows what He is doing! We
should also keep in mind the brevity of life. It will enable us to
maintain a focused view of eternity's values. Prayerfully –
consider these things with me.

To Remember:

Our lives are likened to a vapor
that appears only for a little while
and then vanishes away.
~ James 4:14 ~

(NLT): "Your life is like the morning fog -
it's here a little while, then it's gone."

With eternity's values in view, Lord.
May I do each day's work for Jesus
With eternity's values in view.
~ Alfred B. Smith (1941) ~

41. Abandonment

Perspective and Reality Moment

Robinson Crusoe, a novel by Daniel Defoe, was first published in 1719, and sometimes considered to be the first novel written in English. After a tumultuous journey that sees his ship wrecked by a vicious storm, his lust for the sea remains so strong that he sets out to sea again. This journey also ends in disaster as the ship is taken over by pirates, and Crusoe becomes the slave of a Moor. He manages to escape and years later, he joins an expedition to bring slaves from Africa, but is shipwrecked in a storm about forty miles out to sea on an island which he named the Island of Despair. His companions all die. He proceeds to build a fenced-in habitation near a cave which he had excavated. He keeps a calendar by making marks in a wooden cross that he built. He reads the Bible and suddenly becomes religious, thanking God for his fate in which nothing is missing but society. The immediacy of his situation is the sense of abandonment – having been left completely and finally; forsaken utterly; deserted and alone to either survive by ingenuity or to die in despair. Crusoe chose to live and devised a plan of survival and deliverance from his Island of Despair.

In a similar way, a recent film, *Castaway*, tells the story of Chuck Noland who is a time-obsessed FedEx systems analyst, who travels worldwide resolving productivity problems at FedEx depots. A Christmas with relatives is interrupted by Chuck being summoned to resolve a problem overseas. While flying through a violent thunderstorm somewhere over the southern Pacific Ocean, an incident occurs on Chuck's plane which results in it crashing into the ocean. Chuck is able to escape the sinking plane and is saved by an inflatable life-raft, which floats for some time in the storm before being washed up on an island. It soon becomes clear that the island is uninhabited, and Chuck's early attempts to make visual signals for any searching aircraft, and to escape the island in the remnants of his life raft are fruitless. Four-years pass, and after a large sheet of plastic washes up on the island, Chuck decides to use it as a sail in the construction of a raft. After spending some time building and stocking the raft and deciding when the weather conditions will be optimal, Chuck launches the raft and finally escapes the island. After some time on the ocean, the raft is virtually destroyed by a storm. Distraught, Chuck resigns himself to his fate and abandons his attempt to find rescue. Half-dead and sunburned, he is found drifting a short time later by a passing cargo ship. Upon returning home Chuck discovers that he has long been given up for dead by everyone he knows; his family and friends held a funeral; and the love of his life had married someone else. A deep sadness has now become part of his inner-being and despair. He had hoped for renewed happiness and experienced additional sadness as he attempts to cope with the cost of having been lost and abandoned.

Some situations of abandonment occur by accident, whereas others happen by design. In Genesis 37, there is the account of Joseph being sold into slavery. His older brothers feel he is more loved by their father than they are, and come to the point where they hate him. At first, they plan to kill him but then decide to sell him to a passing caravan. A commentator (James Boice) shares his impressions of Joseph: "Joseph, being seventeen years old: was loved and hated, favored and abused, tempted and trusted, exalted and abased. Yet at no point in the 110-year life of Joseph did he ever seem to get his eyes off God or cease to trust him. Adversity did not harden his character. Prosperity did not ruin him. He was the same in private as in public."

What is it that sustained Joseph in his abandonment? How did he manage to survive rejection, hatred, being alone, and having become chattel in the hands of others? It is the truth shared throughout all generations and eloquently stated in Isaiah 41:10, "Fear thou not, for I am with thee; be not dismayed, for I am thy God; I will strengthen thee; I will help thee; I will uphold thee with the right hand of my righteousness." There comes a time during a famine when Joseph will be in the company of his brothers one more time. They are at his mercy and revenge could be so sweet. But - what will Joseph do at such a moment? How will he respond to those who hated him and wanted him dead? In Genesis 50:19-21, "Joseph said to them…You intended to harm me, but God intended it for good to accomplish what is now being done…And he reassured them and spoke kindly to them." He forgave them and fed them! What would you have done in this situation? How would you have reacted?

Many people find themselves trapped in isolation or abandonment. Some deal with it admirably whereas others allow it to embitter them toward life in general and people in particular. The idea of casting one's burden of loneliness, isolation or abandonment upon the Lord seems foreign to them. If the truth was told, they might express that they feel abandoned by God as well.

Abandonment brought to mind a friend's background. He was writing a note to a talk radio host and shared some intimate details about his life. Part of what he wrote included:

> "My early life involved foster homes, an orphanage and a struggling mother and stepfather. I was in the 9th grade in Junior High School, and worked after school. My two 10th grade brothers also worked after school. We arrived home at the apartment around 10 PM one night, and found a note. 'Boys, we have moved…if we find work we will send for you.' Our parents left us

with no forwarding address. We never heard from them again. I was first arrested in the 5th grade for throwing rocks at a rich neighbor's house. I was in the 8th grade when I mistakenly shot a hole in the floor at a home where I was trying to scare a friend hiding in a closet. I was arrested in the summer of 1951, after finishing the 10th grade, for disrupting a couple in the theater."

This type of real-life experience could be repeated often by other bruised and abandoned individuals. The sad story includes valleys and occasional peaks. The only conclusion is that this friend and his brothers were unwanted and abandoned.

It is vital that one be reminded of what the Lord has said in His Word. Such a person needs to be reminded of what the Lord declared in Isaiah 41:9-10 (NLT), "I have chosen you and will not throw you away. Don't be afraid, for I am with you. Don't be discouraged, for I am your God. I will strengthen you and help you. I will hold you up with my victorious right hand." Don't let adversity or abandonment harden your character. God has not abandoned you! Prayerfully – Consider these things with me.

To Remember:

Good biblical character always
triumphs and survives cultural adversity.

42. A Bridge to Nowhere

Perspective and Reality Moment

Feeling abandoned to the inevitable is the plight of many people. They are caught in the whirlwind of human events and become overlooked or ignored. People find themselves in impossible situations and feel they are trapped, helpless and without a ray of hope in their circumstances. All motivation to go on with life seems lost; hopes have faded; the will to be and to do has dissipated; the personal spirit has been broken or crushed; one seems suspended in time and space – uncared for and abandoned to unwanted and harsh realities. One tries to smile in spite of adversity but the pain of a broken heart prevents the brightness of that smile. What is one to do? How can one escape such complicated circumstances? How did one ever arrive at this point? It is like being on an endless treadmill or traveling on a bridge that goes nowhere – except for the endurance of further affliction, anguish and pain.

The above describes too many lives and marriages. It is a sad case and event of being abandoned to a very difficult context for one's life. What is abandonment? What does it look like? How did it occur? A frequent place where abandonment is observed is in certain marriages. The definition of abandonment is: "to leave completely and finally, forsake utterly, desert; to give up, discontinue, withdraw from…" Synonyms are: abandon, relinquish, renounce, to give up all concern in something; to give up or discontinue any further interest in something/someone because of discouragement, weariness, distaste, or the like…"

Abandonment can occur in several areas, individually, as a family unit, or a particular group (such as military units being taken as prisoner of war). It impacts and crosses several areas of one's being - emotional; physical; financial; fiduciary. Consider these as one feels alone on the bridge to nowhere: The Emotional - where a husband or wife no longer maintains a viable relationship with their spouse's feelings, needs, or self-worth. The Physical - where a spouse no longer maintains a viable interpersonal relationship, or is just not present to demonstrate any responsibility or care; also, one who is being harsh and cruel – abusive. The Financial - where a spouse no longer provides for the upkeep of another; a family; a property; relationships; a total disregard for everyone and everything except self-narcissism run amok. The Fiduciary (a legal or ethical relationship of trust) – where a spouse ignores mortgage responsibilities as a person to whom property or power is entrusted for the benefit of another and where other legal obligations are neglected – this is the DNA of the one who abandons and who has disregarded all duty, responsibility and trust.

In a marriage and family situation, this can imperil the marriage vows where each person (spouse) had vowed loyalty to and oneness with in a forever relationship (until death us do part). The sad reality is that one spouse or the other, perhaps both mutually, will have the sense of being deserted and abandoned – left with hopelessness and despair – on a bridge to nowhere.

The Bible states how the irresponsible and/or abusive spouse is viewed from a heavenly perspective: (First Timothy 5:7-8 – NLT): "But those who won't care for their own relatives, especially those living in the same household, have denied what we believe. Such people are worse than unbelievers." And the same verses in The Message: "Tell these things to the people so that they will do the right thing in their extended family. Anyone who neglects to care for family members in need repudiates the faith. That's worse than refusing to believe in the first place." That being said, what about the abandoned and/or abused person and family? Do they remain on the bridge to nowhere? Will anyone positively care about their plight and need? Who will reach out to encourage and assist?

The Bible speaks of those in a non-marriage situation who found themselves abandoned - trapped - with nowhere to go. There is Jonah in the great fish; Elijah as he fled from the threats of Jezebel; Job when he lost all of his family and possessions; Israel when they disobeyed God and chose idols instead. For these, and others, there was a reality check - their abandonment would end through deliverance by the Lord's hand.

A word of encouragement for the weary, oppressed, abandoned is Isaiah 42:5-6, "This is what God the Lord says, He who created the heavens and stretched them out, who spread out the earth and all that comes out of it, who gives breath to its people, and life to those who walk on it: I, the Lord, have called you in righteousness; I will take hold of your hand. I will keep you..." He will take you from the bridge to nowhere and place you on a road to somewhere. He will hold on to you and never let go of you! He will lead you safely from where you are to a place that is right, safe, wholesome and good for you! Enjoy being in His grip! Have no regrets of where you are when you are securely held in the Master's hand. Prayerfully – Consider these things with me.

To Remember:

In the secular world, you may
have been abandoned;
in the spiritual world, your helplessness
has become hopefulness.
You are safe and secure in the grip (grasp)
of The Master's hand.

43. Misdirected Hope

Hope - what is it and what does it mean to and for you – for us all? Generally, it is the feeling that what I can be will somehow turn out for the best. It does contain an element of fatalism because this type of hope is in a vacuum and lacks any degree of certainty that it can or will come to pass. Life is filled with choices upon which decisions are made in an arbitrary way. Sometimes, in hindsight, the choice that was made is regretted and the alternative is no longer available or viable. We can attempt to be independent as we do the things we have greatest interest in by ourselves and in our own way, or we can realize that being an island unto ourselves is not the wisest or best alternative. Wisdom would dictate that we must have trust and confidence as we depend on someone or something. When it comes to choices and decisions, consideration should always be given to Proverbs 11:14 (ESV) "Where there is no guidance the people fall, but in abundance of counselors there is safety."

In Romans 4:1-2 (ESV), there is an important statement made in regard to Abraham and his hope in someone or something other than himself. The verses state: "What then shall we say was gained by Abraham, our forefather according to the flesh? For if Abraham was justified by works, he has something to boast about, but not before God." God is indicating to Abraham that he and his wife Sarah, even though they are advanced in years, would have an heir. Based upon his faith in the God who never breaks a promise, we note in Romans 4:18, "In hope he believed against hope, that he should become the father of many nations, as he had been told: So, shall your offspring be." The summary of how he arrived at this place of absolute hope is shared in Romans 4:20-21 (NLT), "Abraham never wavered in believing God's promise. In fact, his faith grew stronger, and in this he brought glory to God. He was fully convinced that God is able to do whatever he promises."

The two dynamic phrases in these verses should be an encouragement for each of us, namely, "he never wavered in believing God's promise" and "he was fully convinced that God is able to do whatever He promises." Is this the foundation on which your spiritual life and hope rests? Is this the confidence and hope that motivates you as a follower of Jesus Christ? Have you totally embraced and implemented these things as a reality in and for your life? First Peter 1:3, 13 (NIV) shares this truth: "In his great mercy he has given us new birth into a living hope through the resurrection of Jesus Christ from the dead. Therefore, with minds that are alert and fully sober, set your hope on the grace to be brought to you when Jesus Christ is revealed at his coming."

Misdirected hope will usually be looking to a person rather than to the Lord. One can look to a medical doctor rather than the great physician. One can become dependent on government welfare agencies for provisions rather than on the God Who promised to supply for all one's needs. One can look to the secular society for identity or acceptance rather than to Jesus Christ who instructed (John 15) "Abide in Me" and (John 13:34-35) "by this shall all people know you are My disciples if you have love for one another." In the secular world, we can participate and negotiate for peace rather than accepting the gift of peace offered by the prince of peace, Jesus Christ.

In what and in whom is your hope and confidence? As a clear reminder for the people of his day, Isaiah 26:3-4 (NLT) shared this truth: "You will keep in perfect peace all who trust in you, all whose thoughts are fixed on you! Trust in the Lord

always, for the Lord God is the eternal rock." Prayerfully –
Consider these things with me.

To Remember:

God is always ready, willing, able and
dependable to be your strength and to
provide for all your needs.

44. Inconsequential Indifference

Indifference has several definitions and usages. In part, it means: "having no particular interest or concern; being apathetic not active or involved; not mattering one way or the other; having no marked feeling for or against..." The synonyms are: "mediocre, undistinguished, uninspired, commonplace." It's redundant to connect indifference with that which is inconsequential - seeing life and things as being "of little or no importance; insignificant; trivial; illogical; irrelevant." These words describe one who has become detached from any or all responsibility, and who is resistant to receiving any advice or assistance to become involved in a positive and constructive way in matters pertaining to life, liberty and the pursuit of happiness.

Those who make this their life choice have chosen a vacuum lifestyle rather than a vibrant and productive one. The contrast for many is inferred in the book, *The Greatest Generation*, written by Tom Brokaw. One source puts it into a broader context by referring to – "the lost generation of the 1880s (who fought in World War I) and the silent generation of the 1930s." *The Greatest Generation* is a term coined by journalist Tom Brokaw to describe the generation of Americans who grew up during the deprivations of the great depression, and then went on to fight in World War II. It also makes mention of those whose productivity within the war's home front made a decisive material contribution to the war effort. Some of those who survived the war then went on to build and rebuild the United States industries in the years following the war. Brokaw observes: "this is the greatest generation any society has produced." He argued that the men and women fought not for the fame and recognition, but because it was the right thing to do. When they came back they rebuilt America into a superpower. It seems as though the cycle has now brought us into the emergence of an indifferent generation.

There are two Biblical references that come to mind in this regard. One reference is in First Kings 18 (NIV). Elijah, the Prophet of God, is challenging and entering into a contest with the prophets of Baal. The key is in verse 21, "Elijah went before the people and said, how long will you waver between two opinions? If the Lord is God, follow him; but if Baal is God, follow him. But the people said nothing." In one translation, it states: "the people answered him not a word." When Elijah appeals to the gathered people in terms of their loyalty and commitment, their silence was deafening! They chose to be spectators rather than participants. They would rather observe than to assist. It could've been cowardice – but more likely – it was their posture of inconsequential indifference. The Second reference is in Revelation 3:14-16, "This is the message from the one who is the Amen – the faithful and true witness, the ruler of God's creation: I know all the things you do, that you are neither hot nor cold. I wish you were one or the other! But since you are like lukewarm water, I will spit you out of my mouth!" The head of the Church – Jesus Christ – observes the behavior of the non-committed and indifferent – and declares they are distasteful and useless to Him. The act of expectoration (spitting) by Jesus is one of consequence and judgment. It is the presence of a tepid and detached attitude (matter-of-fact manner, indifference) toward God.

One of the idioms of the English language allows for the phrase – "sit on the fence". Basically, it's implication is: "not to take sides in a dispute; not to make a clear choice between two possibilities (such as, the image of someone straddling a fence, representing indecision)." Some of us grew up hearing the phrase: "If you stand for nothing, you will fall for anything!" It is tremendously important to have firm convictions in terms of what one believes. Know what the Bible teaches and believe it. For too long, people have operated within their self-imposed limitation of several idioms: "don't rock the boat"; or "just get along with everyone"; *ad nauseum*. This can cause one to fall into the state of being obsequious: "showing servile complaisance or deference." The synonyms are: "cringing, submissive." Does Jesus Christ look at you and your lifestyle choices and say: "...you are neither hot nor cold. I wish you were one or the other"?

An example is when the children of Israel are preparing to move into their inheritance. Before they do, Joshua issued a challenge to the people of Israel. In Joshua 24:19-22 (NIV), there is a dialogue between Joshua and the people: "Joshua said to the people: You are not able to serve the Lord. He is a holy God; he is a jealous God. He will not forgive your rebellion and your sins. If you forsake the Lord and serve foreign gods, he will turn and bring disaster on you and make an end of you, after he has been good to you. But the people said to Joshua: No! We will serve the Lord. Then Joshua said: You are witnesses against yourselves that you have chosen to serve the Lord. They replied: Yes, we are witnesses." Joshua gave his own testimony, commitment and affirmation in Joshua 24:14, "If serving the Lord seems undesirable to you, then choose for yourselves this day whom you will serve, whether the gods your ancestors served beyond the Euphrates, or the gods of the Amorites, in whose land you are living. But as for me and my household, we will serve the Lord."

Joshua epitomized that which the Lord was requiring in the Book of Revelation. All of us are here to fulfill God's purpose for and in our lives. The choice is obvious: "Be hot – and – not cold!" This is what we are to do and be! You need

to make the commitment to just do it! You'll never regret it!
Prayerfully – Consider these things with me!

To Remember:

One should choose today
who or what he will serve.

45. Algorithms

Perspective and Reality Moment

An algorithm is understood and utilized in a variety of ways, by putting it in the context of the methods employed to divide and conquer (D&C). The American Heritage Dictionary defines Algorithm as: "A step-by-step problem-solving procedure, especially an established, recursive computational procedure for solving a problem in a finite number of steps." For instance, "In computer science…a D&C algorithm works by recursively breaking down a problem into two or more sub-problems of the same or related type, until these become simple enough to be solved directly. The solutions to the sub-problems are then combined to give a solution to the original problem." Simply stated, algorithm is understood by the following: "divide and conquer is a powerful tool for solving conceptually difficult problems. All it requires is a way of breaking the problem into sub-problems, of solving the trivial cases and of combining sub-problems to the original problem."

The divide and conquer (D&C) approach is not limited to mathematical and scientific issues alone. If one pays attention, D&C is often a political ploy used by a man or woman seeking an elected office, or in the effort to gain support for legislation. An example of this is in the health care reform debate and possible legislation. At the time of the discussion and debate, one might've have heard the Speaker of the House state that people are coming to town halls with swastikas. Others have likened the citizens attending town halls employing terms such as – brown shirts, mobs, extremists. One office holder has on his webpage: "right-wing domestic terrorists"! The headline of a published article at that time was: Planned Phone Campaign on 9/11 Against 'Right-Wing Domestic Terrorists' On Health Reform." Plain and simple, it is the divide and conquer technique.

"United We Stand, Divided We Fall," is a favorite phrase, used in varying forms, of political orators from Benjamin Franklin to Abraham Lincoln. It has been attributed to Aesop, both directly in his fable The Four Oxen and the Lion and indirectly from The Bundle of Sticks. It gained some popularity after John Dickinson's 'Liberty Song' was published on July 18, 1768, in the Boston Gazette. The work contained the lines: "Then join in hand, brave Americans all— By uniting we stand, by dividing we fall!" Patrick Henry was passionate in this regard and used the phrase in his last public speech, given in March 1799, in which he denounced The Kentucky and Virginia Resolutions. Clasping his hands and waving his body back and forth, Henry declaimed, "Let us trust God, and our better judgment to set us right hereafter. United we stand, divided we fall. Let us not split into factions which must destroy that union upon which our existence hangs." At the end of his oration, Henry fell into the arms of bystanders…Two months afterward he was dead.

Abraham Lincoln, a wise President during the sad and dark days of the Civil War, agonized over the nation. He empathized and emphasized the sentiments of Patrick Henry – "United We Stand, Divided We Fall." Sadly, the trend of the contemporary culture is to marginalize and fractionalize. It may bring momentary gain, but ultimately, it will prove to have contributed greatly to the ruin and demise of a once great and Christian nation.

In the spiritual sense, Jesus prayed for His followers so that they would not divide or be conquered. He did not want his followers to be marginalized and fractionalized. His Prayer is recorded in John 17:20-23, "My prayer is not for them alone. I pray also for those who will believe in me through their message, that all of them may be one, Father, just as you are in me and I am in you…" There is also the prayer offered by Paul in Ephesians 4:2-6, "Be completely humble and gentle; be patient, bearing with one another in love. Make every effort to keep the unity of the Spirit through the bond of peace. There is one body and one Spirit - just as you were called to one hope when you were called - one Lord, one faith, one baptism; one God and Father of all, who is over all…through all…in all." If you have committed yourself to Jesus Christ, this should be – must be - your goal and reality – "united we stand – divided we fall!" Prayerfully - consider these things with me!

To Remember:

Unity and freedom in Christ should never be blurred.

46. Immediately

Perspective and Reality Moment

We live in a culture that is confused about the basics of life. There is considerable misunderstanding about getting priorities for life transacted immediately versus a developing cultural norm regarding instant gratification. Instant gratification overrides anything immediate because personal pleasures have greater appeal than the fulfillment of priorities requiring immediate attention. Anything immediate seems to be foreign to those absorbed in a narcissistic culture. Delay and procrastination have become common-place for those who lack a sense of urgency. Delay will never make any demanding situation acceptable or remedied. The mentality has developed within society that one can get around to it without specificity of when or how. Chosen to be forgotten is the definition of the word immediate: "without lapse of time; without delay; instantly; at once." It is interesting that the antonym for immediate is "later."

When Jesus Christ began His earthly ministry, He chose disciples to be part of His ministry. The nature and substance of the call is in Matthew 4:18-22: "As Jesus was walking beside the Sea of Galilee, He saw two brothers, Simon called Peter and his brother Andrew. They were casting a net into the sea, for they were fishermen. Come, follow Me, Jesus said, and I will make you fishers of men. And immediately - at once - they left their nets and followed Him. Going on from there, He saw two other brothers, James son of Zebedee and his brother John. They were in a boat with their father Zebedee, mending their nets. Jesus called them - and immediately – at once - they left the boat and their father and followed Him."

There was something urgent about the call of Jesus that brought about the immediate and at once response.

Compare the "immediate" and "at once" response of the disciples with Luke 14:15-20 when an invitation had been proffered to attend a great banquet. Jesus mentions some invited guests who had other things they wanted to do and places they wanted to be. They resorted to making excuse why they could not attend. They could've altered their schedule and attended but they made a choice to do other things – lesser things – and declined the invitation. This type behavior paves the way for other similar decisions to be wade. How does this type of thinking allow irresponsibility to surface and become a norm? It occurs because of what one wants to do and when he wants to do it. It is a very self-serving orientation.

In September 2013, James Emery White published a paper on the Culture of Complacency in the Church. It included:

> "Complacency has to do with self-satisfaction, a sense of contentment regarding the state of things. And it all starts with complacency in a leader. Now, most leaders would say, I am anything but complacent! I know. That's the problem. No one thinks they are complacent." He then goes on to share and discuss the Five Marks of Complacency. They are: (1) Being far too easily satisfied. (2) Being too quick to make excuses, (3) Allowing that one never has enough time. (4) Being no longer teachable. (5) Being content with early success.

What is the very least one should do by way of focus, priorities and commitment? How will one's efforts (or lack of the same) be measured by the Lord? What is His minimum requirement? Starting point one: Micah 6:8, "The Lord has told you what is good, and this is what he requires of you: to do what is right, to love mercy, and to walk humbly with your

God." Starting point two: Psalm 37:5-6, "Commit your way to the Lord; trust in him, and he will act." Starting point three: Proverbs 16:2-3, "All the ways of a man are pure in his own eyes, but the Lord weighs the spirit. Commit your work to the Lord, and your plans will be established."

Excuses rather than an immediate response were deemed by those offering them to be acceptable and reasonable. Their mentality was sometime but not immediately, and personal self-interest rather than honoring the preparer of the banquet feast and table. Some of the above excuses are similar to the five excuses offered by Moses in Exodus 3 and 4 when God had chosen him to lead His people out of bondage. Moses responded to God: (1) 3:11-12, Who am I? (2) 3:13-15, I don't have authority! (3) 4:1-9, The people won't believe me! (4) 4:10-11, I lack the ability to carry out this assignment! (5) 4:12-17, Send someone else, please. I just do not feel equal to the task and even if I did, I don't want to be the one to do it.

Just think if Peter and Andrew, James and John had responded by offering an excuse to Jesus and His calling of them to be His disciples. There is a sharp distinction between immediate and at once when compared with excuses to attend a banquet or lead God's people out of their captivity. How do you respond to opportunities to serve your Lord and Master? Maybe you think you have "all your ducks in a row" and don't need these reminders. Are you content to be a "get-a-round to it" type person or do you respond by the action of immediate and at once? Prayerfully – consider these things with me.

To Remember:

"Now" never means later and
"today" never means tomorrow.

47. Being Free Indeed

Perspective and Reality Moment

A great truth of the Gospel is that one who has been enslaved to sin can be set free from that bondage and live in the liberty secured once for all in Jesus Christ. The truth of the Gospel is that one can be unchained, unshackled and unfettered from bondage and slavery to sin. The key is to seek Jesus Christ who is the only one who can cause those chains to fall off so you can be free indeed. He was emphatic and clear when He stated His eternal purpose in John 8:31-34 (NLT), "You are truly my disciples if you remain faithful to my teachings. And you will know the truth, and the truth will set you free...I tell you the truth, everyone who sins is a slave of sin. A slave is not a permanent member of the family, but a son is part of the family forever. So, if the Son sets you free, you are truly free." The familiar Hymn, "Amazing Grace" had some slight changes made by Chris Tomlin to include: "My chains are gone, I've been set free My God, my Savior has ransomed me...Unending love, Amazing grace."

Jesus has removed the chains that bound one and immediately brought about the needed reality of being set free indeed. If one tries to loosen the shackles by which he is bound, he will find it to be a frustrating effort that will result in failure. The force and power of the enemy is too great for an ordinary person to overcome. At some point, if being free indeed is that which one seeks, the need to turn to the only one who can set one free indeed must be sought. Even though it may be challenging and confusing, the first step of faith alone must be taken. When one responds to the invitation of Jesus Christ to come to Him, deliverance by grace alone will occur, and Jesus Christ will not turn that one away.

An additional passage that underscores the truth regarding slavery to sin and being set free is Hebrews 2:9-18 (BSB),

> "But we see Jesus…He too shared in their humanity, so that by His death He might destroy him who holds the power of death, that is, the devil, and free those who all their lives were held in slavery by their fear of death…"

A contemporary worship chorus has a simple and very meaningful repetitious lyric that includes the step of faith for the one who will Come to Jesus. A portion of that lyrics is, "Weak and wounded sinner, Lost and left to die…Come to Jesus…Come to Jesus and live!" When one comes to Jesus, the chains that once bound will be loosed forever. This will begin the new walk and new life. It will mean old things passing away and all things becoming new. One will be free indeed because Jesus Christ accomplished that freedom for all who will believe in Him. Begin to live the new life in Christ by living in the truth and reality of Galatians 5:1, "It is for freedom that Christ has set us free. Stand firm, then, and do not be encumbered once more by a yoke of slavery." Even though one may be an extraordinary situation, or be confronted with overwhelming challenges, God's grace is always more than sufficient for it (Second Corinthians 12:9). We also assured that in addition to His grace, His strength will enable one to bear the burden and do whatever needs to be done through God's strength alone (Philippians 4:13). Therein is where one will find both peace and contentment. Prayerfully – consider these things with me.

To Remember:

Jesus Christ alone paid the price
that sets one free indeed.

47. Being Free Indeed

He redeemed - He bought us –
out of our slavery and bondage to sin.

48. Victorious Christian Living

Perspective and Reality Moment

Victorious Christian Living, is it needed by twenty-first century followers of Jesus Christ? Is it possible to attain it in the twenty-first century Church? While reading a chapter of a soon to be published book on the subject: Christian Living – Intentional or Accidental? – some interesting thoughts surfaced. A question posed for the reader to consider was apt: Are you living the intentional Christian life, or a life that is more accidental and haphazard?

Years ago, an emphasis for Christian living was referenced as The Victorious Christian Life movement. The strong influence was promoted by, The Torchbearers and the Keswick Movement (both operated out of Great Britain). Part of the emphasis was to learn to live above one's circumstances rather than to be bogged down under them. The goal of Torchbearers (founded by Major Ian Thomas) was to provide practical Christian education designed to develop personal spiritual growth. It also had in view the preparation of people for a functional and effective life through the Church. To accomplish the goals entailed development and increase of one's knowledge of the Bible.

The Keswick Movement had a twofold emphasis. Justification is by the grace of God, and sanctification is by the indwelling of the Holy Spirit in one's life. The early influence of the Movement was based upon the teachings of John Wesley and Adam Clarke. Other Christian leaders became involved in the Keswick Movement, such as the missionary, Hudson Taylor of the China Inland Mission and the devotional writer, Oswald Chambers. The emphasis of both groups that resonated most was the need for holiness in one's life.

On a personal basis, in my earliest acquaintance with both groups, three verses captured my attention and focus. The first was Philippians 1:21, "For to me to live is Christ and to die is gain." This was often connected to Romans 12:1-2 and the need for one to learn and implement the concept of presenting one's own self to the Lord to become a living sacrifice offered to Him. The second verse that resonated and influenced my focus was II Chronicles 20:15, "Do not fear or be dismayed...for the battle is not yours but God's." It related to the need for one to implement Hebrews 12:2 and to, "Keep on looking to Jesus" and not the baggage that often accompanies one's life and the circumstances by which one is often surrounded. The third verse was Hebrews 12:14, "Pursue...holiness, without which no one will see the Lord." The sobering words regarding holiness and hope of entering God's heaven are clear. The words are stated as they are because that is precisely what the Lord is requiring.

The picture Isaiah had of heaven is recorded in Isaiah 6:3-4. "The seraphim were calling to one another: Holy, holy, holy is the Lord Almighty; the whole earth is full of his glory. At the sound of their voices the doorposts and thresholds shook and the temple was filled with smoke." This connects nicely to First Peter 1:15-16 and serves as a constant reminder and requirement: "Just as He who called you is holy, so be holy in all you do, for it is written: Be holy, because I am holy." This same requirement is indicated in the Sermon on the Mount, Matthew 5:48 (BSB), "Be perfect, therefore, as your Heavenly Father is perfect."

This emphasis was and has to be with the lifestyle choice one makes and the relationship one chooses to develop. The precise requirement for a Biblical follower of Jesus Christ is stated in Second Corinthians 6:14, "Do not be yoked together with unbelievers. For what do righteousness and wickedness have in common?" The equally obvious answer is that there is no common ground. It is either Christ and the Gospel, or rejection and unbelief. It is either righteousness or wickedness. Which of these contrasts identify who and what you are? Prayerfully – consider these things with me.

To Remember:

Seeking the Kingdom of God first
must be intentional and not accidental.
~ Matthew 6 ~

49. Pondering

Perspective and Reality Moment

Pondering is considering something deeply, thoroughly, thoughtfully, and meditating upon it for a period of time. In terms of spiritual growth and commitment, how much time does one spend pondering the Almighty God - who He is and what He does? A Hymn of worship, Praise to the Lord, the Almighty, enjoins one to: "Ponder anew what the almighty can do, Who with His love doth befriend thee!" How often do you ponder what the almighty will do?

The *Westminster Shorter Catechism* #1 asks: What is the chief end of man? The response is: Man's chief end is to glorify God and enjoy Him forever. One way for this to be accomplished is the application of Hebrews 13:15-16, "Through Jesus, therefore, let us continually offer to God a sacrifice of praise, the fruit of lips that confess His name. And do not neglect to do good and to share with others, for with such sacrifices God is pleased."

There can be serious consequences for those who fail to glorify God and enjoy him forever. God is serious and He wants us to take Him seriously and to heed His Word in all areas of life. The Lord raised a vital issue with His people in Hosea 4:6, when He said to them: "My people are destroyed for lack of knowledge; because you have rejected knowledge, I reject you...And since you have forgotten the law of your God, I also will forget your children." One generation can have a negative impact on succeeding generations. The Lord also shares with His people that which will delight Him, Jeremiah 9:23-24, "Thus says the Lord: Let not the wise man boast in his wisdom, let not the mighty man boast in his might, let not the rich man boast in his riches, but let him who boasts boast in this, that he understands and knows me, that I am the Lord who practices steadfast love, justice, and righteousness in the earth. For in these things I delight, declares the Lord."

Another opportunity for pondering is shared in the *Heidelberg Catechism* question and answer for Lord's Day #1: "What is thy only comfort in life and death?" The response is very compelling and moving: "That I with body and soul, both in life and death, am not my own, but belong unto my faithful Savior Jesus Christ; who, with his precious blood, has fully satisfied for all my sins, and delivered me from all the power of the devil; and so preserves me that without the will of my heavenly Father, not a hair can fall from my head; yea, that all things must be subservient to my salvation, and therefore, by his Holy Spirit, He also assures me of eternal life, and makes me sincerely willing and ready, henceforth, to live unto him." In this response, it is obvious there is much one can and should ponder about the mercy and provision of God for one of His own. We could go through the response phrase by phrase and ponder anew what the Almighty will do and has done. Then, we can exclaim with the angels, Praise to the Lord, the almighty, the King of creation.

Do you have a prepared checklist for your personal devotional time with the Lord? There are variations for what it should contain. One practical starting point would be making use of The Navigator's Prayer Hand plan. In their introduction to The Prayer Hand, they state: It is an easy way to remember five essential aspects of prayer: confession, petition, intercession, thanksgiving and praise." Their recommendation is: "Pray through each of these five purposes, using the Prayer Hand to walk you through each one. Remember that prayer is ultimately about aligning our own hearts with God's." It is a beginning point along the narrow way to spend time pondering God.

Obviously, we need to spend more quality time with God as we ponder Him and His greatness and as we ponder His

will for us individually and each of us who follow Him
corporately. Prayerfully - consider these things with me.

To Remember:

Keep looking only and always to Jesus
and always take a serious God seriously.
Hebrews 12:1-2

50. Destined to Be Holy

Perspective and Reality Moment

In the devotional, *My Utmost for His Highest*, September 1, 2017, Oswald Chambers reminds the reader of First Peter 1:16, "It is written: Be holy, for I am holy." He goes on to write:

> "We must continually remind ourselves of the purpose of life. We are not destined to happiness, nor to health, but to holiness. Today we have far too many desires and interests, and our lives are being consumed and wasted by them. Many of them may be right, noble, and good, and may later be fulfilled, but in the meantime God must cause their importance to us to decrease. The only thing that truly matters is whether a person will accept the God who will make him holy. At all costs, a person must have the right relationship with God."

He proposes two questions for consideration:

"Do I believe I need to be holy? Do I believe that God can come into me and make me holy?"

The devotional closes with these thoughts:

> Holiness means absolute purity of your walk before God, the words coming from your mouth, and every thought in your mind— placing every detail of your life under the scrutiny of God Himself. Holiness is not

simply what God gives me, but what God has given me that is being exhibited in my life.

There can be many questions raised about the subject of holiness: How important should Holiness be in a person's life? Why is it a necessary requirement for all of God's people? Can there be degrees of Holiness? If I, along with all other followers of Jesus Christ, are holy as God is holy, won't we be viewed as clones or robots? Some answers were given by Jerry Bridges in his book, *The Pursuit of Holiness.*

On January 1, 2012, *Tabletalk*, a publication of Ligonier Ministries interviewed Jerry Bridges and asked him: What do you see as the greatest need in the church today? He responded:

> I would say the most fundamental need is an ever-growing awareness of the holiness of God. The emphasis of my own ministry has been the believer's personal pursuit of holiness. But years ago, I came to realize the gospel has to be the foundation and motivation for the pursuit of holiness. Believers need the gospel to remind them that our standing with God is not based on our own obedience but on the perfect, imputed righteousness of Christ. Otherwise, the pursuit of holiness can be performance driven: that is, 'If I'm good, God will bless me.

It is helpful to remember some of the basic truths of God's Word and His expectation for His people and followers. First Corinthians 1:2 defines the calling of God and what it necessitates: "To the church of God that is in Corinth, to those sanctified in Christ Jesus, called to be saints together with all those who in every place call upon the name of our Lord Jesus Christ, both their Lord and ours." The operative phrases are: "to those sanctified in Christ Jesus" and followed immediately by "called to be saints." The Oxford Dictionary defines saint as: "A person acknowledged as holy or virtuous and regarded in Christian faith as being in heaven after death."

In Romans 1:1-7 (ESV), Paul focuses on the importance of holiness and that which God had in mind for those who are called to be saints: "Concerning his Son...who was declared to be the Son of God in power according to the Spirit of holiness by his resurrection from the dead. To all those who are loved by God and called to be saints: Grace to you and peace from God our Father and the Lord Jesus Christ." Once again, there is the linkage of holiness and all those who are called to be saints. At the very least, the plan of God for each of His children is that they reflect His holiness. His people are to be examples of the viability of the Gospel. Accordingly, all who name the name of Jesus Christ are expected to live exemplary lives.

What are some things that should be included in an exemplary life? Ephesians 4:21-24 (NLT) gives us a starting place: "Since you have heard about Jesus and have learned the truth that comes from him, throw off your old sinful nature and your former way of life, which is corrupted by lust and deception. Instead, let the Spirit renew your thoughts and attitudes. Put on your new nature, created to be like God— truly righteous and holy." Colossians 3:8 (NLT) adds: "Now is the time to get rid of anger, rage, malicious behavior, slander, and dirty language." A key word in this listing is "now" that suggests it must be done without any further delay. If one pauses and reflects upon the words of Colossians 3, it would be easy to conclude that the wardrobe for God's elect is being shared. It is not a suggestion for one to try in a hit or miss manner but an identifying character trait and quality that is be common for all those who are God's children – called to be saints. There needs to be an avoidance of picking and choosing which part of the overall garment of holiness will be worn. It is one of those requirements that is all or none. Prayerfully – consider these things with me.

To Remember:

Delay and procrastination
are tools and devices of the devil.
Resist them (and him) steadfastly
is a requirement - not an arbitrary suggestion.

51. Vanishing Values

Perspective and Reality Moment

In each generation, writers address church growth factors and how a group can be more successful as they grow their church. Some also point out that the church as a whole is dying. They speak of the "Nones" and "Dones" people groups to illustrate their point. Some choose to ignore and shrug off these thoughts and statistics. A person can Google Search for data about reasons why the health of some churches is declining. One website is Pastoral Care, Inc. where some reasons are given. In their "Statistics in Ministry", they indicate: 70% of pastors constantly fight depression; 70% do not have someone they consider a close friend; 50% of pastors feel so discouraged that they would leave the ministry if they could, but have no other way of making a living; 50% of the ministers starting out will not last 5 years; the profession of "Pastor" is near the bottom of a survey of the most-respected professions, just above "car salesman"; 4,000 new churches begin each year and 7,000 churches close; over 1,700 pastors left the ministry every month last year; over 3,500 people a day left the church last year; many denominations report an empty pulpit crisis. They cannot find ministers willing to fill positions; the number one reason pastors leave the ministry - church people are not willing to go in the same direction and with the same goal of the pastor and are not willing to follow or change.

The radicalization within the culture is affecting the thinking and behavior of people both in the culture as well as in the Church. All types of groups are publicly voicing opinions and participating in protests about cultural issues and government activity. At times, it appears that chaos is victorious. David expressed his concerns in Psalm 11:1-3 (NIV), "I trust in the Lord for protection. So why do you say to me: Fly like a bird to the mountains for safety! The wicked are stringing their bows and fitting their arrows on the bowstrings. They shoot from the shadows at those whose hearts are right. The foundations of law and order have collapsed. What can the righteous do?"

David responded to his own question, Psalm 11:4-7, "But the Lord is in his holy Temple; the Lord still rules from heaven. He watches everyone closely, examining every person on earth. The Lord examines both the righteous and the wicked. He hates those who love violence…The righteous Lord loves justice. The virtuous will see his face." This is the hope of all whose faith and confidence is in the Lord alone. Will the culture and radicalization win the day? No! The Lord is always victorious and enables us to walk and live in His triumph. He will build His Church and the gates of hell will not prevail against it (Matthew 16:18). Prayerfully – consider these things with me.

To Remember:

Jesus Christ is the only sure foundation
and we are secure in Him.

52. Godly Character

Perspective and Reality Moment

Martin Luther King, Jr. is remembered by some of the words he used in his speeches. One statement pertained to "the content of one's character." What does that content mean and what should it include? Generally, it means: "The combination of features and traits that form an individual's nature or traits; as well as one's moral or ethical qualities." It seems as though character and personal integrity are vital to each other. If integrity is not present, it affects how one is viewed as an individual.

Several years ago, in a pastoral effort, I met with a graduate from one of the reformed seminaries in the hope that he and his wife would become part of the Church Plant ministry being conducted. His immediate reply was that all people, both within and outside of the Church, are dysfunctional. Instead of exploring why he was convinced and embracing his view, I erred by challenging his failure to consider the redemptive work of Jesus Christ and the transforming grace of God who not only redeems but Who also begins the edification and sanctification process within the individual. I referenced Second Corinthians 5:17, "If anyone is in Christ, he is a new creation; old things pass away and behold, all things become new." My emphasis was upon the reality that the dysfunction could be transformed into being functional in Jesus Christ. Those who had been purposeless can become people of purpose in Christ. If this is not possible or likely, then there is no basis for hope in Christ. The young man held to his dysfunctional convictions and I continued to hold the transformational potential and possibilities.

I find great comfort in the words of First Corinthians 6:9-11, that delineates between the dysfunctional and the functional; between those steeped in trespasses and sins, and those who have been redeemed:

> "Do you not know that the wicked will not inherit the kingdom of God? Do not be deceived: Neither the sexually immoral, nor idolaters, nor adulterers, nor men who submit to or perform homosexual acts, nor thieves, nor the greedy, nor drunkards, nor verbal abusers, nor swindlers, will inherit the kingdom of God."

It would be sad and hopeless if that's where the context ended. However, Paul continued and stated:

> "And that is what some of you were. But you were washed, you were sanctified, you were justified, in the name of the Lord Jesus Christ and by the Spirit of our God."

> There's the transformation from dysfunctional to functional. The key words being: "you were washed, you were sanctified, you were justified."

The obvious point Paul is making is twofold: (a) "that is what some of you were" and (b) "but you were washed, sanctified, justified in the name of the Lord Jesus Christ." It reminds us that the marvelous grace of Jesus is greater than all of our sin. It reminds us there is always hope for the hopeless. It reminds us that God's love, mercy and grace far exceeds one's intellect and/or ability to comprehend. As the old evangelists would often remind their audiences: "The grace of God can save from the gutter-most to the uttermost." As one yields to Jesus Christ, the character of Christ begins to become their character. The Holy Spirit fills us with the fruit of the Christ-like nature and being (Galatians 5:22-24). Prayerfully – consider these things with me.

To Remember:

God is still able to make
all things new in your life – starting today!
Invite Him into your life
to fashion and mold you into all of what
He wants you to be – for Him.

53. Biblical Revival

Perspective and Reality Moment

Living in the south (the Bible Belt, as it was once called and known) has advantages and disadvantages. One advantage is that there is occasion to see a tradition being continued in various Church groups. Most have seen the signs that declare – Church Revival – three nights only (or some similar statement). While the intention seems noble, the idea conveyed that something unique, supernatural or dynamic will occur during those selected days is short-sighted. Question: Can a revival be announced or is it something that takes place spontaneously? What is God's requirement for revival?

It is the better part of wisdom that one should never drift too far from a specific word from the Lord in this regard. After the completion of the Temple being built, it is recorded in Second Chronicles 7:12-15 (NIV),

> Then the Lord appeared to Solomon in the night and said to him: I have heard your prayer and have chosen this place for myself as a house of sacrifice. When I shut up the heavens so that there is no rain, or command the locust to devour the land, or send pestilence among my people, if my people who are called by my name humble themselves, and pray and seek my face and turn from their wicked ways, then I will hear from heaven and will forgive their sin and heal their land. Now my eyes will be open and my ears attentive to the prayer that is made in this place.

An additional factor emphasized is upon prayer. The Lord said: "I have heard your prayer." One can wonder why prayer for church renewal or revival is so seldom prayed. One would do well to follow the model in Acts 4:29-31,

"And now, Lord, look upon their threats and grant to your servants to continue to speak your word with all boldness, while you stretch out your hand to heal, and signs and wonders are performed through the name of your holy servant Jesus. And when they had prayed, the place in which they were gathered together was shaken, and they were all filled with the Holy Spirit and continued to speak the word of God with boldness."

Another observation is that the "Revival" posters and signs are usually associated with Baptist or Pentecostal-oriented church groups. Some Presbyterian Churches have benefitted from instruction based upon From Embers to A Flame by the Presbyterian Pastor Harry L Reeder. He states: "God's instructions to the church at Ephesus serve as a curriculum outline for church revitalization and vitality: "Remember therefore from where you have fallen, and repent and do the deeds you did at first." In Revelation 2:5. "There is a three-fold paradigm for renewing our churches: Remember, Repent, Recover! Church revitalization or vitality is nothing more than following God's prescription for church health. Church health naturally leads to conversions and improved personal discipleship, for our good and God's glory." Does the Church you attend need a Biblical and spiritual awakening, revival, renewal, revitalization – or - a proper burial? Prayerfully – consider these things with me.

To Remember:

We are in desperate need for the Spirit of God
to descend upon our hearts and the church – today!

53. Biblical Revival

A Prayer:

Spirit of the living God
fall fresh on me;
break me, melt me, mold me, fill me.
Spirit of the living God fall fresh on me.
~Iverson ~

54. Backing Up

Perspective and Reality Moment

My father-in-law was twenty-five years older than my mother-in-law. During their courtship, he loaned her his Pierce-Arrow automobile so she could drive fifty miles from Chattanooga, TN to Menlo, GA to visit her parents. She knew how to drive forward but she was unable to back up. Fortunately, at the farm, there was ample room to maneuver the car, so backing up in that instance was not an issue.

One of the challenging areas for the professing Christian is the ability to back up carefully and gracefully. Some hard-chargers are like a snow plow being driven rapidly and snow/ice is splattering the landscape. It may accomplish passage in a driving lane but it has piled the snow and ice in such a way that driveways and crosswalks are blocked. Some parked cars become trapped in a growing snow bank. Just as the snow plow cannot reverse its action, even so the professing Christian cannot easily reverse his course of action. It becomes easy to say that the parked car should have been moved before the plowing began. Lame excuses are often utilized to rationalize an action taken or a statement made. Chuck Swindoll wrote in Insights for Today - May 17, 2016:

"Wouldn't you love the ability to go back in time and change something you did or said? I know there have been moments in my life—awful moments when I acted on the impulse of the flesh—that I would dearly love to call back. But alas, I cannot. The sad fact is, we cannot go back. None of us can. We cannot undo sinful deeds or unsay sinful words. We cannot reclaim those moments when we were possessed by rage, lust, cruelty, indifference, or hard-headed pride...we must live with the consequences of our words and our actions. What we sow, the Scriptures warn, we will also reap (Galatians 6:7)."

Jesus shared an important principle in the Sermon on the Mount, Matthew 5:24-25, "If you are offering your gift at the altar and there remember that your brother has something against you, leave your gift there before the altar. First go and be reconciled to your brother; then come and offer your gift." How often have you seen this principle both embraced and implemented? A further step in reconciliation is stated by Jesus in Matthew 18:15-17.

Is it possible that the Word of God is being selectively believed and practiced? It seems obvious that in this area and several others there is a need to back up and do that which Jesus Christ taught and directed His followers to do. Another of the hindrances to backing up is one's pride. It is almost impossible to admit one was wrong and to apologize for it. Sadly, it is equally difficult to forget the words that had been exchanged or particular actions that had been taken. Maintaining biblical character and being sensitive to other people and the hurt that may have been inflicted upon them is difficult to recognize and even more difficult to admit to an offended party.

James 1:22-24 shares an important character comparison and consideration: "Be doers of the word, and not hearers only. Otherwise, you are deceiving yourselves. For anyone who hears the word but does not carry it out is like a man who looks at his face in a mirror, and after observing himself goes away and immediately forgets what he looks like." Has the church and Christian inadvertently quenched the Spirit by failing to do God's Word (inspired by the Holy Spirit)? Prayerfully – consider these things with me.

54. Backing Up

To Remember:

If you believe God's Word
then you must always do what it says –
promptly and satisfactorily.

55. Thought Control

Perspective and Reality Moment

I recently read a devotional thought that suggested we need to be reprogrammed with truth. Reprogrammed is an interesting word. It has several possibilities but it conveys this basic purpose, it is "a plan of action designed to accomplish a specified end; a schedule of activities and procedures that are to be followed." Another tool used for thought control is often referenced as brainwashing: "A method of systematically changing attitudes or altering beliefs." Brainwashing was often used in totalitarian countries where torture, drugs or psychological-stress techniques were employed. It is generally any method of controlled systematic indoctrination usually based on repetition or confusion.

The Biblical approach to thought control is suggested in the following Scriptures: Second Corinthians 10:4-5 (ESV): "For the weapons of our warfare are not of the flesh but have divine power to destroy strongholds. We destroy arguments and every lofty opinion raised against the knowledge of God, and take every thought captive to obey Christ." Romans 12:2 (ESV): Be transformed by the renewal of your mind, that by testing you may discern what is the will of God, what is good and acceptable and perfect." Psalm 119:105-106 (ESV): "Your word is a lamp to my feet and a light to my path. I have sworn an oath and confirmed it, to keep your righteous rules." Philippians 4:8-9 (ESV): "Whatever is true, whatever is honorable, whatever is just, whatever is pure, whatever is lovely, whatever is commendable, if there is any excellence, if there is anything worthy of praise, think about these things. What you have learned and received and heard and seen in me, practice these things, and the God of peace will be with you." The significant phrase in Philippians 4:9 is: "practice these things."

Most of us are acquainted with the illustration of a visitor to New York City who was desirous of going to Carnegie Hall to hear a concert. When he asked a stranger how he could get to Carnegie Hall, the stranger told him: practice, practice, practice. The application is obvious. If Philippians 4:8 is to become the reality of our thoughts and lives, the way to reach that objective is the implementation of Philippians 4:9 – or - practice, practice, practice.

Joseph Stowell commented, September 3, 2017 in Get More Strength for the Journey:

- We need to know what to do with our time, energy, and money.
- We need to know what to do with our minds.
- We need to be taught what to do about friends and how to handle enemies.
- We need to be taught about family, work, and leisure.
- How can one begin to think adequately and properly before God?
- What is it that a child of God must do in order to think correctly?
- Is it a complicated set of rules one must follow?
- How can the average person begin to grow spiritually and Biblically?
- Is there a basic principle that must be followed?

The answer and place to start is shared in Colossians 3:2 (ESV), "Set your minds on things that are above, not on things that are on earth." The NLT paraphrases this verse: "Think about the things of heaven, not the things of earth." This is the only correct pathway, narrow though it may be, for the Biblical Christian's desire to think the thoughts that are always pleasing to the Lord and Savior, Jesus Christ. Prayerfully – consider these things with me.

To Remember:

God's Word is jam-packed
with time-tested principles of success
for every situation and issue of life.
~ Joseph Stowell ~

56. Beyond Expectation

Perspective and Reality Moment

The English language, sentence structure and use of nuance can be both challenging and humorous. This is the case with the use of the *Paraprosdokian* (something beyond expectation). It is a figure of speech in which the latter part of a sentence or phrase is surprising or unexpected in a way that causes the reader or listener to reframe or reinterpret the first part. It is frequently used for humorous or dramatic effect. There are examples of *paraprosdokian* (taken from Patriot Humor/The Patriot Post).

In a proverbial sense, it is stated: As the tree falls, so shall it lie; As a man lives, so shall he die; As a man dies, so shall he be; Through all the eons of eternity.

In sentence structure, some possibilities are:

- Do not argue with an idiot. He will drag you down to his level and beat you with experience.
- I want to die peacefully in my sleep, like my grandfather. Not screaming and yelling like the passengers in his car.
- Light travels faster than sound. This is why some people appear bright until you hear them speak.
- If I agreed with you, we'd both be wrong.
- War does not determine who is right - only who is left.
- Knowledge is knowing a tomato is a fruit; Wisdom is not putting it in a fruit salad.
- The early bird might get the worm, but the second mouse gets the cheese.

- Evening news is where they begin with "good evening," and then proceed to tell you why it isn't.
- To steal ideas from one person is plagiarism. To steal from many is research.
- A bus station is where a bus stops. A train station is where a train stops. My desk is a work station.
- How is it one careless match can start a forest fire, but it takes a whole box to start a campfire?
- Dolphins are so smart that within a few weeks of captivity, they can train people to stand on the very edge of the pool and throw them fish.
- I thought I wanted a career; turns out I just wanted paychecks.
- A bank is a place that will lend you money if you can prove that you don't need it.
- Whenever I fill out an application, in the part that says "If an emergency, notify:" I put "DOCTOR."
- A clear conscience is usually the sign of a bad memory.
- Always borrow money from a pessimist. He won't expect it back.
- Hospitality: making your guests feel like they're at home, even if you wish they were.
- Money can't buy happiness, but it sure makes misery easier to live with.
- Some cause happiness wherever they go. Others whenever they go.
- Nostalgia isn't what it used to be.
- Change is inevitable, except from a vending machine.

A biblical example of *paraprosdokian* can be gleaned from Ecclesiastes 11 (NLT):

Verse 3: When the clouds are heavy, the rains come down. When a tree falls, whether south or north, there it lies.
Verse 4: If you wait for perfect conditions, you will never get anything done.
Verse 8: When people live to be very old, let them rejoice in every day of life. But let them also remember that the dark days will be many. Everything still to come is meaningless.
Verses 9-10: Young man, it's wonderful to be young! Enjoy every minute of it. Do everything you want to do; take it all in. But remember that you must give an account to God for everything you do. So, banish grief and pain, but remember that youth, with a whole life before it, still faces the threat of meaninglessness.

Verses that have always elicited reflection – although simple, they are also profound and cause one to reread them: First John 5:11-13, "This is the testimony that God gave us eternal life, and this life is in his Son. Whoever has the Son has life; whoever does not have the Son of God does not have life. I write these things to you who believe in the name of the Son of God that you may know that you have eternal life." There is a constructive wisdom one can attain that will result in knowledge that is based upon truth. No *paraprosdokian* (nothing surprising or beyond expectation) in Scripture - just basic truth! Prayerfully consider these things with me!

To Remember:

Always keep your talking and speaking
simple, purposeful, basic and understandable.

57. Respect

A general news story in 2017 records the following: "The Cleveland Browns made pre-season headlines last month for a non-football related reason: twelve of their players refused to stand for the national anthem during a pre-season game, one of the biggest NFL-related anthem protests to date. Now, Cleveland-area first responders are firing back. In the wake of the protest, area-first responders say that if football players don't want to respect America, the American flag and the national anthem then they aren't going to hold a large field-size American flag during the national anthem at the Browns' first game this season." The issue for the first responders: "if football players don't want to respect America, the American flag and the national anthem…" - it is a failure to respect part of what is foundational to the nation.

As protests take place across the country, one can observe the symbols of the past being desecrated and torn down; the Flag of the United States of America being torn, trampled on and burned; businesses being vandalized and looted; historic statues are being toppled or removed; authority figures – first responders, police and firefighters are becoming the target for objects being thrown at them, disrespected, disobeyed and sometimes shot at; elected officials speaking with generalized "fluff" in an attempt to identify with an angry mob of protesters when it would be best if they remained silent. One gets a sense of the tone of helplessness in Psalm 11:3(ESV) "if the foundations are destroyed, what can the righteous do?"

Overall, there is a broader area of disrespect when it comes to the levels of authority and to the elders who are part of the population. There is a premise of the Lord that is being ignored in this country and culture. One can read it in Leviticus 19:32 (NASB), "You shall rise up before the gray-headed and honor the aged, and you shall revere your God; I am the Lord." This is a mandate of our Lord. Is it being heard, obeyed, implemented adequately today? Sadly, the answer is – No! The NLT paraphrases this verse: "Stand up in the presence of the elderly, and show respect for the aged. Fear your God. I am the Lord."

What does it mean to show respect? On the webpage, vocabulary.com, the definitions given are: "People respect others who are impressive for any reason, such as being in authority, like a teacher or policeman, or being older like a grandparent." You show respect by being polite and kind. For a lot of people, taking your hat off is a show of respect. When people are insulted, or treated badly, they feel they haven't been treated with respect. You can respect things as well as people, such as saying the pledge of allegiance to the flag of the United States of America and showing respect to your country.

Respect is: "to regard highly, to think much of." Romans 13:7 (ESV) enjoins one to: "Pay to all what is owed to them: taxes to whom taxes are owed, revenue to whom revenue is owed, respect to whom respect is owed, honor to whom honor is owed." In the brashness of youth and young adults, they have convinced themselves that anyone older or in a position of authority must earn their respect. While they are sadly mistaken, a reason for their error may be attributable to the fact that God is being ignored in our schools and culture. In their ignorance and rebellion, the younger generation goes on disobeying the Lord and destroying foundational principles as they protest and insist on removing symbols of our historic heritage.

The prevailing question of the Psalmist (11:3) – what can the righteous do? – must be answered by word and action. The guiding principle is stated in Proverbs 14:33-34 (ESV),

"Wisdom rests in the heart of a man of understanding, but it makes itself known even in the midst of fools. Righteousness exalts a nation, but sin is a reproach to any people."

The obvious tension at this point is "in the midst of fools" and the emphasis upon "righteousness exalts". Will it be an easy task? No! Why? Because in the midst of fools, the emphasis upon righteousness will continued to be ignored. A description of the attitude and mindset of the fool at this point is stated in Proverbs 14:6-9,

> "The mocker seeks wisdom and finds none, but knowledge comes easily to the discerning. Stay away from a fool, for you will not find knowledge on their lips. The wisdom of the prudent is to give thought to their ways, but the folly of fools is deception. Fools mock at making amends for sin, but goodwill is found among the upright."

While the task may be formidable and difficult, there is a word of encouragement for those who are willing to run the risk of being light amid the onslaught of darkness. Will such a one be warmly and readily received and heard? Most likely, no! Will such a one be insulted and disrespected as the Gospel and message of righteousness is spoken? Probably, yes! However, the words of encouragement and hope shared in First Corinthians 1:25-30 (ESV) should be considered:

> "For the foolishness of God is wiser than men, and the weakness of God is stronger than men. For consider your calling, not many of you were wise according to worldly standards, not many were powerful, not many were of noble birth. But God chose what is foolish in the world to shame the wise; God chose what is weak in the world to shame the strong; God chose what is low and despised in the world, even things that are not,

to bring to nothing things that are, so that no human being might boast in the presence of God. And because of him you are in Christ Jesus, who became to us wisdom from God, righteousness and sanctification and redemption."

Hope should be taken with the intended distinction implied in the inclusive phrase "not many" rather than the exclusive that "not any" are called. This is why we are to labor on. We will not know the length of the battle before us for the souls of men. We do know it will be arduous and demand full commitment of all who follow the true leader, Jesus Christ. We are willing to make the total commitment because of the assurance given in First Corinthians 15:57 (BSB), "But thanks be to God, who gives us the victory through our Lord Jesus Christ." Prayerfully – consider these things with me.

To Remember:

Go, labor on: spend, and be spent,
thy joy to do the Father's will.
It is the way the Master went;
should not the servant tread it still?
~ Horatius Bonar ~

58. Philosophy of Ministry

Perspective and Reality Moment

A previous chapter (Chapter 25) considered whether or not the Church is waxing or waning? Another way of considering that question is to ask whether or not the church is having any measurable impact in the church and culture or has it become an organization with a limited appeal to a specific people group? When a church is seeking a pastor, they usually have a list of questions for and about the candidate. Some are borne out of the particular church's vision for ministry whereas others copy questions from some other church's group and ask them of their candidate and those who are contacted for reference about their candidate.

An example copied from one questionnaire asked: "Which demographic in the church does he find it easiest to work with? Which demographic does he find the most difficult to work with, and how does he try to meet the needs of all? Question: How should a Pastoral Candidate answer that question? How should one who is a reference answer the same question? For better or for worse, I answered it in the following way:

Wow! That is a vague and leading question. He (the candidate) is not overly concerned about the social status of an individual or family. Also, he is an adaptable man and willing to advance cross-cultural ministry, as well as ministry to all. If I was the candidate, this is a question I would be asking of the Pulpit Search Committee: How adaptable is the session (ruling elders) and church family? Would they invite a person of a different race to come to church with them? What about a former prisoner? Would they invite such a one into their home for a fellowship meal or small group Bible study? Would anyone entering your church have the sense of be accepted and belonging? Why? Why not?

I would have expanded that in the in-person interview to look into the faces of the pulpit search committee and ask them additional questions based upon their having raised the one about demographics. Some of my questions: (a) What have you been doing by way of on-going cross-cultural ministry? (b) Are people of other ethnic backgrounds welcomed into this church and fellowship? (c) Is that welcome genuine? (d) What is the church's approach to people of lesser means and status? Are they welcomed into the church and fellowship? Do they feel accepted, wanted and needed? Do some prominent (and wealthy) members (or leaders) view them as being trailer-park-white-trash, or lesser people because of their skin color?

Will it make some search committee members and congregants feel uncomfortable? Yes! Might some of them cringe rather than give a response? More than likely, they would. But then, one further question/thought: Isn't it hypocritical to have an expectation of what a pastor should be if some of the church search committee and church members are not being or doing it themselves? This may be the reason why Jesus addressed hypocrisy in Matthew 23:23-24 (NIV),

"Woe to you, teachers of the law and Pharisees, you hypocrites! You give a tenth of your spices—mint, dill and cumin. But you have neglected the more important matters of the law—justice, mercy, (humility) and faithfulness. You should have practiced the latter, without neglecting the former. You blind guides! You strain out a gnat but swallow a camel."

Because of a developing habit of forgetting some of the things the Lord wants His people to remember and practice, it might also be appropriate to give consideration to that which the Lord made known in Micah 6:6-8 (NIV),

> "With what shall I come before the Lord and bow down before the exalted God? Shall I come before him with burnt offerings, with calves a year old? Will the Lord be pleased with thousands of rams, with ten thousand rivers of olive oil? Shall I offer my firstborn for my transgression, the fruit of my body for the sin of my soul? He has shown you, O mortal, what is good. And what does the Lord require of you? To act justly and to love mercy and to walk humbly with your God."

In both Micah 6 and Matthew 23, the Lord is addressing the empty rituals and the games people tend to play in and with religion. To the Scribes and Pharisees, Jesus made thus very point throughout Matthew 23 as He pronounced the woes upon them:

> Woe to you, scribes and Pharisees, you hypocrites! You shut the kingdom of heaven in men's faces. You yourselves do not enter, nor will you let in those who wish to enter.
> Woe to you, scribes and Pharisees, you hypocrites! You traverse land and sea to win a single convert, and when he becomes one, you make him twice as much a son of hell as you are.
> Woe to you, blind guides! You say, 'If anyone swears by the temple, it means nothing; but if anyone swears by the gold of the temple, he is bound by his oath.
> Woe to you, scribes and Pharisees, you hypocrites! You pay tithes of mint, dill, and cumin, but you have disregarded the weightier matters of the Law: justice, mercy, and faithfulness.

Woe to you, scribes and Pharisees, you hypocrites! You clean the outside of the cup and dish, but inside they are full of greed and self-indulgence.

Woe to you, scribes and Pharisees, you hypocrites! You are like whitewashed tombs, which look beautiful on the outside, but on the inside, they are full of dead men's bones and every impurity.

Woe to you, scribes and Pharisees, you hypocrites! You build tombs for the prophets and decorate the monuments of the righteous. And you say, 'If we had lived in the days of our fathers, we would not have been partners with them in shedding the blood of the prophets.

Jesus was pointing out to them that they were not serious about true religion nor that which the Lord required. They were actively manipulating the Scriptures for their personal power and privilege. If Jesus assessed your religious practices, how would He assess them? How serious are you in terms of your relationship to the Lord and His requirements? How faithfully do you embrace them for His people and servants? Prayerfully – consider these things with me.

To Remember:

My life, my love, I give to Thee,
Thou Lamb of God who died for me;
Oh, may I ever faithful be,
My Savior and my God!
~ R.E. Hudson ~

59. Self-Righteousness

Perspective and Reality Moment

The Holy Scriptures clearly state those things that are repugnant to the holy and eternal God. They are listed in various ways such as (Galatians 5:19-21), "The acts of the flesh are obvious: sexual immorality, impurity, and debauchery; idolatry and sorcery; hatred, discord, jealousy, and rage; rivalries, divisions, factions, and envy; drunkenness, carousing, and the like. I warn you, as I did before, that those who practice such things will not inherit the kingdom of God." Elsewhere (Colossians 3:5-9), a similar list states: "Put to death, therefore, the components of your earthly nature: sexual immorality, impurity, lust, evil desires, and greed, which is idolatry. Because of these, the wrath of God is coming on the sons of disobedience. When you lived among them, you also used to walk in these ways. But now you must put aside all such things as these: anger, rage, malice, slander, and filthy language from your mouth. Do not lie to one another, since you have taken off the old self with its practices"

Overall, two of the major sins that are committed by many professing Christians are the sin of comparison and the sin of self-righteousness. It allows them to think and believe they are not as bad as those described in the above verses. As a matter of fact, they arrive at a place where they actually feel superior, even more credible, spiritual and righteous, to those with whom a comparison is being made. They think of themselves as one who embraces some good works that outweigh any negatives that others practice. This type of thinking allows one to miss the indicting words spoken in Daniel 5:22,27: "But you, Belshazzar…have not humbled yourself, though you knew all this…You have been weighed on the scales and found wanting." Just pause and reflect upon what it means to be weighed in God's scales and to have fallen short of measurement accuracy. It indicates that it has become routine to avoid, ignore and evade the words of Romans 3:10, "There is no one righteous, not even one." And, the words of Isaiah 64:6 (NLT), "We are all infected and impure with sin. When we display our righteous deeds, they are nothing but filthy rags." It has become common to pretend and employ self-vindication that we have surpassed this assessment of God and His scales.

A devotional I read daily (Get More Strength for the Journey) posed a series of heart-searching and convicting questions:

- Would the worst of sinners feel loved by you, or would they sense that you are more likely to condemn and ostracize them?
- Has your goodness become a habit, or does it thrive as a response of love and gratitude for all that Jesus has done for you?
- Do you feel like you have been forgiven much? Why, or why not?
- Are you genuinely touched when you sing the words, "He saved a wretch like me," or does the term "wretch" refer to someone else?"
- Is righteousness a possibility for anyone at all?
- Is it achievable for someone like me?

Paul wrote in Second Corinthians 5:15,21 (ESV): "Jesus Christ died for all, that those who live should no longer live for themselves, but for Him who died for them and was raised again... God made Him who knew no sin to be sin on our behalf, so that in Him we might become the righteousness of God." Are you living your life for Him who died for you and rose again? Is there observable evidence that you are becoming the righteousness of God? Prayerfully consider these things with me.

To Remember:

Not I, but Christ be seen
in every deed and action of mine.
~A.B. Simpson ~

60. The Unneeded

Perspective and Reality Moment

A devotional in *Our Daily Bread* concluded and summarized with these words: "James, a New Testament writer, challenged Christ-followers saying: "pure and lasting religion in the sight of God our Father means that we must care for orphans...in their troubles" (James 1:27 - NLT). We live in a day when, like those first-century orphans, children of every social strata, ethnicity, and family environment are at risk due to neglect, human trafficking, abuse, drugs, and more. How can we honor the Father who loves us by showing His care for these little ones Jesus welcomes?" It is an urgent and vital question due to the number of aborted and abandoned babies and children.

A ministry begun several years ago is the Big Oak Ranch in Alabama. They have made a home for many abandoned children. Their stated goal for the ministry to the children is: We make four promises to every child that comes to the Ranch:

1. We love you (love and emotional support).
2. We will never lie to you (truth and honesty).
3. We will stick with you until you're grown (security).
4. There are boundaries; don't cross them (discipline).

From that foundation, they raise every child to know God's love.

A noted Christian Philosopher, Francis Schaefer, offered some practical, encouraging and pious counsel when he said: With God, there are no big people and no little people. There are either consecrated people or non-consecrated people. In the book, Realizing Significance, I wrote about people who were relegated to a status of being expendable, unwanted and unneeded. They are usually ignored and often passed by.

When reading the words of James, other questions come to mind:

(1) Who will run the risk and pay the price to reach out to care for the unwanted and abused?

(2) Is prayer and financial contribution the response James and Jesus were speaking of and suggesting?

(3) How would you define tangible ways to make a difference with the unwanted, abused and neglected?

What is the observation, assessment and requirement of Jesus Christ in reaching out to the unwanted and unnoticed? Matthew 25:34-40 states that which is most important to Him in this regard: "Then the King will say to those on his right (the sheep): Come, you who are blessed by my Father; take your inheritance, the kingdom prepared for you since the creation of the world. For

(a) I was hungry and you gave me something to eat;

(b) I was thirsty and you gave me something to drink;

(c) I was a stranger and you invited me in;

(d) I needed clothes and you clothed me;

(e) I was sick and you looked after me;

(f) I was in prison and you came to visit me.

Then the (Biblically) righteous will answer him: Lord,

- When did we see you hungry and feed you?
- Or thirsty and give you something to drink?
- When did we see you a stranger and invite you in?
- Or needing clothes and clothe you?

- When did we see you sick or in prison and go to visit you?

The King will reply: Truly I tell you, whatever you did for one of the least of these brothers and sisters of mine, you did for me."

It is of great importance to determine how you have responded to the heart and words of Jesus Christ. Were His words ingested and embraced by you? When will you respond and show His care for/to the unwanted? Do the things that matter to the Lord matter to you? How will Jesus respond to those who ignore His words and refuse to act as He wants them to do? In Matthew 25:44-46 (NLT), He answers: "And they will go away into eternal punishment, but the righteous will go into eternal life."

How will you respond to "one of the least of these"? Can you feign lack of knowledge before the Lord who knows one's thoughts, deeds and actions? Are you one who is more apt to rationalize, procrastinate and obfuscate (confuse or make unclear) the precise words of Jesus Christ to His people? Can you – will you commit yourself to make a difference in the life of "one of the least of these"? Is there anyone you consider to be off-limits as a recipient of ministry done in the name of the Lord? Is it because of some unnamed or unmentioned characteristic of a person? Reverse this process and place yourself in the position of those who are deemed unwanted, unnecessary or unneeded. How would you feel, if you sensed the need for acceptance by someone, if you were consistently passed by? What would you want done about it? Prayerfully consider these things with me.

To Remember:

A Prayer - Lord, help me to see what you see
and to care about who and what You care about.

James Perry

Lord, make me an instrument of your peace,
Where there is hatred, let me sow love;
where there is injury, pardon; where there is doubt, faith;
where there is despair, hope; where there is darkness, light;
where there is sadness, joy;
O Divine Master, grant that I may not so much seek
to be consoled as to console; to be understood as to
understand; to be loved as to love. For it is in giving that we
receive; it is in pardoning that we are pardoned;
and it is in dying that we are born to eternal life.
~ The Prayer of Frances of Assisi ~

61. Becoming Calloused

Perspective and Reality Moment

There are all kinds of exploitation and individual subjugation (enslavement) taking place throughout the world. There is human exploitation; suppression and oppression of various people groups; abandoned and unwanted children; orphanages; and street people.

In a devotional, Sin's Cure, (September 14, 2017), Dr. A. W. Tozer was quoted as having written the following:

> Had Hitler been a good and gentle man, six million Jews now dead would be living; had Stalin been a Christian, several million Russian farmers would be alive who now molder (slowly decay and disintegrate) in the earth. Consider the thousands of little children who died of starvation because one man had a revengeful spirit; think of the millions of displaced persons who wander over the earth even today unable to locate mother or father or wife or child because men with hate in their hearts managed to get into places of power; think of the young men of almost every nation, sick with yearning for home and loved ones, who guard the empty wastes and keep watch on frozen hills in the far corners of the earth, all because one ruler is greedy, another ambitious; because one statesman is cowardly and another jealous.

If we look at the way professing Christians treat one another and the apparent indifference within the structured church, it should not be surprising that the groups identified as the "Nones" and "Dones" have dropped out of the culturally-oriented church. They have wearied of the forms and worship modifications and adaptations. They see it more as form without purposeful function. If function is somewhat present, they have come to believe that they have been relegated to being a spectator rather than a participant.

When the church was wrestling with the issue of glossolalia (speaking in an unknown language), the apostle Paul asked a very poignant and rhetorical question in First Corinthians 14:8, "If the trumpet sounds a muffled call, who will prepare for battle?" The NLT renders this verse: "If the bugler doesn't sound a clear call, how will the soldiers know they are being called to battle?" Could the indiscernible bugle sound be the current cause for negative reaction within the cultural-oriented church today? In terms of the speaking in another tongue issue, Paul also wrote in First Corinthians 14:39-40, "So, my brothers, be eager to prophesy and do not forbid speaking in tongues. But everything must be done in a proper and orderly manner." The general theme of the Chapter 14 suggests that one should neither seek to speak in an unknown tongue nor should one forbid those who are speaking in another tongue. At one point, A.B. Simpson (former Presbyterian Minister) had his views on this subject printed in pamphlet form with the title, Seek Not, Forbid Not. The fuller explanation can be read by going to: The Christian and Missionary Alliance webpage (See link below) that contains views of both Simpson and A.W. Tozer on the gifts of the Holy Spirit.

Another factor that enters into the overall indifference is how easily indifference can drift into callousness on the part of professing Christians and the churches they nominally support. Paul wrote to Timothy and reminded him of a stark reality within organized religion, Second Timothy 3:1-9, "In the last days, terrible times will come...For men will be lovers of themselves...having a form of godliness but denying its power...always learning but never able to come to a knowledge of the truth...They are depraved in mind and disqualified from the faith." In First Timothy 1:5-6, Paul shares this cautionary word: "The goal is love, which comes from a pure heart and a good conscience and a sincere faith. Some have departed from these and have turned to meaningless talk."

This is also indicated in Second Timothy 4:3-4, "For the time will come when people will not put up with sound doctrine. Instead, to suit their own desires, they will gather around them a great number of teachers to say what their itching ears want to hear. They will turn their ears away from the truth and turn aside to myths." Could it be that we have arrived at this point and some don't even recognize it nor are they aware of where we are and how we got there? Prayerfully – consider these things with me.

To Remember:

A Promise Keepers Prayer Chorus
Refiner's Fire
Purify my heart, let me be as gold and precious silver.
Purify my heart, let me be as gold, pure gold.
(Chorus)
Refiner's fire, my heart's one desire
Is to be... holy; Set apart for You, Lord.
I choose to be... holy;
Set apart for You, my Master, ready to do Your will.
Purify my heart,
Cleanse me from within and make me holy.
Purify my heart, cleanse me from my sin,
deep within.
~ Brian Doerksen ~

(https://www.cmalliance.org/about/beliefs/perspectives/spiritual-gifts).

62. Name-Droppers

Perspective and Reality Moment

The American essayist, Joseph Epstein, once defined name-dropping as: "using the magic that adheres to the names of celebrated people to establish one's superiority while at the same time making the next person feel the drabness of his or her own life. Name-dropping is a division of snobbery, and one of the snob's missions is to encourage a feeling however vague of hopelessness in others."

Another general description is: "name-dropping is used to position oneself within a social hierarchy. It is often used to create a sense of superiority by raising one's status. By implying (or directly asserting) a connection to people of high status, the name-dropper hopes to raise his or her own social status to a level closer to that of those whose names he or she has dropped, and thus elevate himself or herself above, or into, present company."

There are many other possibilities of intent for the one oriented to being a name-dropper. The basic idea is the attempt of one driven by a desire for recognition and acceptance in a special or select group. This can also occur if person A is sharing with person B a particular article that has been written by person C. Person B is apt to interrupt person A to relate that he has met person C and spoken with him. This may have little or nothing to do with the aforementioned article but it demonstrates that person B wants to appear superior to person A. What is the basis and purpose? To gain a posture of superiority over another.

This causes one to wonder how all of this fits into God's desire and requirement for His people. Where should a person B type fit into God's requirement for personal behavior? In simple, clear and precise words, the correct act of devotion and sincerity is stated (Micah 6:8): "He has told you what is good; and what does the Lord require of you but to do justice, and to love kindness, and to walk humbly with your God? To be a name-dropper sets one in a contrary position to God's requirement to: "walk humbly with your God." Basically, we are being told that it should not be about you because it should be all about Him.

Paul captured this significance and shared his focus and determination in Philippians 3:7-11,

> Whatever gain I had, I counted as loss for the sake of Christ... that I may know him and the power of his resurrection, and may share his sufferings, becoming like him in his death, that by any means possible I may attain the resurrection from the dead.

The only acceptable "name-dropper" utterance should be that Jesus Christ is my Lord. Nothing and no one else should be allowed to come before Him and one's focus upon Him. Is there a remedy for the name-dropper? If a transformation occurs and Christ alone becomes first and foremost in one's life, how will the former name-dropper be received among his peers? Should that be a determining factor in the surrender of the name-dropper to be a Jesus Christ only person? Does the person's life demonstrate this change has occurred? If you have made such a change in your life, will you be received by the body of believers as you walk humbly with your God? The answer should be – Yes! Prayerfully - Consider these things with me!

To Remember:

God's glory should always outweigh man's,
as well as my own self-seeking glory.

63. Artificial Intelligence

Perspective and Reality Moment

From 2011 to 2016, CBS produced the television series, Person of Interest, a science-fiction crime drama. It featured an ex-assassin and a wealthy programmer whose mission is to save lives via computer surveillance – Artificial Intelligence - that sends them the identities of civilians involved in impending crimes. The idea of the program was to intercept that "person of interest" and change the pending negative outcome with a positive result.

In 2007, Stanford University Computer Science Department did an extensive study on artificial intelligence. They concluded:

> "Artificial Intelligence (AI) is the science and engineering of making intelligent machines, especially intelligent computer programs. It is related to the similar task of using computers to understand human intelligence, but AI does not have to confine itself to methods that are biologically observable. Intelligence is the computational part of the ability to achieve goals in the world. Varying kinds and degrees of intelligence occur in people, many animals and some machines."

The study went on to state the obvious:

> "Computer programs have plenty of speed and memory but their abilities correspond to the intellectual mechanisms that program designers understand well enough to put in programs...The matter is further complicated by the fact that the

cognitive sciences still have not succeeded in determining exactly what the human abilities are…this demonstrates that the program designers lack understanding of the intellectual mechanisms required to do the task efficiently."

Is there a Biblical viewpoint regarding intelligence versus artificial intelligence? Jeremiah 9:23-24 (ESV) indicates, "let not the wise man boast in his wisdom, let not the mighty man boast in his might, let not the rich man boast in his riches, but let him who boasts boast in this, that he understands and knows me, that I am the Lord who practices steadfast love, justice, and righteousness in the earth. For in these things I delight, declares the Lord."

An additional thought from Isaiah 29:13-14 (NIV), "These people…their worship of me is based on merely human rules they have been taught…I will astound these people with wonder upon wonder; the wisdom of the wise will perish, the intelligence of the intelligent will vanish."

Lastly, First Corinthians 2:7-10(a), "We declare God's wisdom, a mystery that has been hidden and that God destined for our glory before time began. None of the rulers of this age understood it, for if they had, they would not have crucified the Lord of glory. As it is written: What no eye has seen, what no ear has heard, and what no human mind has conceived the things God has prepared for those who love him - these are the things God has revealed to us by his Holy Spirit." How does God view all of the AI (artificial intelligence) explorations and conclusions? In First Corinthians 3:19-20, "For the wisdom of this world is folly with God. For it is written: He catches the wise in their craftiness," and again: "The Lord knows the thoughts of the wise, that they are futile." Prayerfully consider these things with me.

63. Artificial Intelligence

To Remember:

You should always ask the Lord to teach you
His way and to guide you in it at all times.

64. Adversarial Ambitions

Perspective and Reality Moment

For the people of God in the first century church, the times were sobering and severe. It was a time of fear, threat and upheaval. Persecution was taking place by the dictate of the Emperor of Rome against biblical Christians. Out of necessity, they were being scattered into other provinces that were not yet hostile to them. They left behind their homes and most of their possessions. They could carry very little with them as they fled, that which they had accumulated and saved.

The first reason for persecution came when fires broke out in Rome during the summer of A.D. 64 when Nero was Emperor (A.D. 54-67). He confiscated private property whenever he pleased, executing those who resisted. The fires resulted from Nero's dream of rebuilding Rome into a monument to his greatness. He envisioned great palaces, temples and marble buildings. The fires destroyed about 40 percent of the city. His belief was that the fires and rebuilding the city would be met with approval and personal popularity. When that did not occur, he chose to blame the cause of the fires on the Christians in Rome. The government began to arrest and cruelly tortured believers. During this time of persecution, Nero's minions hunted down and executed Peter and Paul because they had been defined as sect leaders.

Later in the first century, another Emperor, Domitian (A.D. 81-96), instituted a more severe persecution. He saw Christianity as an unlicensed religion and ordered its persecution in A.D. 91. This persecution arose partly because of Domitian's insistence that he be recognized as deity prior to his death. Additionally, he disdained Jews and hated anything Jewish. Since Christianity had Jewish roots, the persecutions included Christians as much as Jews. During Domitian's persecution of the Jews and Christians, the aged Apostle John was banished to the Isle of Patmos. In this time of exile, he had the visions that were written down and became the Book of Revelation in the Holy Scriptures. Many of his words in Revelation bear directly on the intensity of Domitian's persecution. John wrote (Revelation 17:5-6), "Babylon the great, the mother of prostitutes (harlots) and of the abominations of the earth. I saw that the woman was drunk with the blood of God's holy people, the blood of those (the martyrs) who bore testimony to Jesus."

For the difficult times being endured by Jewish believers, Peter wanted them to live, act and deal appropriately. He urged them to be cognizant of the basic reality that there is an adversary who is relentless and ruthless in his desire to destroy the church and all Christians. The words of hope and challenge were stated by him in First Peter 5:6-11 (ESV),

> "Humble yourselves, therefore, under the mighty hand of God… casting all your anxieties on him, because he cares for you. Be sober-minded; be watchful. Your adversary the devil prowls around like a roaring lion, seeking someone to devour. Resist him, firm in your faith… And after you have suffered a little while, the God of all grace, who has called you to his eternal glory in Christ, will himself restore, confirm, strengthen, and establish you. To him be the dominion forever and ever. Amen."

Are you prepared to face a similar challenge and resist any adversary of your day? Will you be committed to Jesus Christ and fight the good fight of faith for His name and glory? Your expectation should be in Jesus Christ alone regardless of any cost or sacrifice. Great challenges should evoke greater commitment and resistance.

Many years ago, while living in St. Louis, MO, we took our young children to the St. Louis Zoo. A lioness had given birth to a litter of cubs and they were on display in the Lion House. The cubs were in a playpen near the zookeeper's office. They were playful and looked cuddly. While the spectators were viewing the cubs, the lioness was nervously stalking back and forth in her cage and roaring very loudly. Doubtlessly, it was all she could do to be protective of her cubs. The lion house seemed to tremble with her loud roaring. Our eldest daughter was about four years of age and amid the roaring of the lioness, she became frightened and ran toward me and leaped into my arms, hugging me tightly about my neck. In her father's arms, she felt protected and safe. The verses above, especially 8-9, have a forceful application for all of us in all generations: "Be sober-minded; be watchful. Your adversary the devil prowls around like a roaring lion, seeking someone to devour. Resist him, firm in your faith."

How do you react to the adversary's stalking and roaring like a lion? In a spiritual sense, where do you feel the safest? Who is your refuge and protector? Do you have any fear of the adversary's capability and design for the human race? At such a moment, do you run to your Heavenly Father and leap into His strong arms and hug Him tightly around His neck? Do you seek Him immediately for His strength, protection and safety?

The question needing an answer is: Are you prepared and ready to respond to the adversary's confrontations and challenges? If so, how, when and in what way? One practical beginning point is: What does the Bible mean to you right now? How well and how much do you honor it daily? In Jeremiah 15:16, we get a glimpse of the prophet's quiet moment when he is alone with the Lord. Jeremiah said: "Your words were found, and I ate them, and your words became to me a joy and the delight of my heart, for I am called by your name, O Lord, God of hosts."

We are not required literally to eat the pages of our Bibles. We are, however, to consume the words of Scripture as we ingest its meaning and application. It should result in our cherishing God's Word in our heart and life. When Jesus prayed for his followers, John 17:17, it was in terms of how they were to use God's Word and how it was to impact their lives. That same prayer is applicable to all Biblical Christians today: "Sanctify them in the truth; Your Word is truth." To be sanctified in the truth of God's Word assumes one will be saturating the Word of God faithfully and consistently. One's life cannot be lived in the abstract or in a vacuum. God's Word must be the lamp for our feet and the light for our pathway. We are to be nourished by it and knowledgeable of it. We are to live it, know it and make it known. Prayerfully consider these things with me.

To Remember:

How should I approach the Bible?
Think of it carefully; study it prayerfully!
Deep in your heart let its oracles dwell!
Ponder its mystery; slight not its history.
For none ever loved it too fondly or well!

65. Unity

Perspective and Reality Moment

World Net Daily posted a column by Patrick Buchanan on August 25, 2017 with the Headline: What Still Unites Us? The viewpoint shifts dramatically and becomes grim when he writes:

> The insight attributed to Alexis de Tocqueville – 'America is great because she is good, and if America ceases to be good, she will cease to be great' – was a belief shared by almost all. What makes our future appear problematic is that what once united us now divides us. While Presidents Wilson and Truman declared us to be a 'Christian nation,' Christianity has been purged from our public life and sheds believers every decade. Atheism and agnosticism are growing rapidly, especially among the young. Traditional morality, grounded in Christianity, is being discarded. Half of all marriages end in divorce. Four-in-10 children are born out of wedlock. Unrestricted abortion and same-sex marriage – once regarded as marks of decadence and decline – are now seen as human rights and the hallmarks of social progress. Tens of millions of us do not speak English. Where most of our music used to be classic, popular, country and western, and jazz, much of it now contains rutting (crude and vulgar) lyrics that used to be unprintable. Where we used to have three national networks, we have three 24-hour cable news channels and a thousand websites that reinforce our clashing beliefs on morality, culture, politics and race."

Culturalism has burst on the scene and replaced Christianity as the focus of an increasingly decadent society. The biblical church used to operate with certain values and foundational principles, such as: John 13:34-35 (BSB), "A new commandment I give you: Love one another. As I have loved you, so also you must love one another. By this all men will know that you are My disciples, if you love one another." Is this what the culture observes about the Church – about you? Too often, the Church is known in communities and other organizations as being dysfunctional, diverse, divisive, or controlled by persons of influence and prominence.

Regarding the believers who had followed Him, Jesus prayed: John 17:20-21 (BSB), "I am not asking on behalf of them alone, but also on behalf of those who will believe in Me through their message, that all of them may be one, as You, Father, are in Me, and I am in You. May they also be in Us, so that the world may believe that You sent Me." Does the culture, world, or church at large manifest that for which Jesus prayed? Do you? Are the Biblical believers one in the Triune God? Is oneness a consistent reality? If there are differences, is effort made immediately to bring about remedy and resolve (as per Matthew 5:23-25 and Matthew 18:15-17)? Church ministers may speak about these things, even preach series on them but do they make any effort to do what Jesus Christ taught? If the idea of pedagogy and preaching is: "It is more caught than taught!" – what has been "caught" by a vast cross-section of church members lately? One Ruling Elder in a Presbyterian Church shared with me that he personally gets little to nothing out of attending a church service. When asked "why?", his response was that the praise band was so loud that he could not even hear himself singing much less anyone around him. If that is true, what is taking place with the "caught" and "taught" concept? What can be "caught" if the decibel level is close to deafening? Are you teachable and eager for in-action learning? If you have listened intently to the Word of God as it was preached, what have you "caught" lately? Prayerfully consider these things with me.

To Remember:

If there is to be unity in keeping with the prayer of Jesus Christ, humility must also be present, real and observable.

66. Excuses and Blame

Perspective and Reality Moment

When was the most recent time you've heard someone accept blame for failure of any sort? The politician blames the other political party; an employee in any occupation blames a co-worker; a student blames an inadequate teacher/professor; a clergyman blames church officers or some member of the church; the Doctor blames incompetent staff; a criminal blames the crime victim or arresting officer. The protestors in the streets of this nation make use of unsubstantiated accusations. At the root of the protests is to find someone or something to blame. The blame game list is long as it approaches the never-ending mindset of excuses.

In some incidents where an accident report was given to the Police or Insurance Company, the following humorous responses were offered as an acceptable reason for the accident:

- Coming home I drove into the wrong house and collided with a tree I don't have.
- I pulled away from the side of the road, glanced at my mother-in-law and headed over the embankment.
- As I approached an intersection a sign suddenly appeared in a place where no stop sign had ever appeared before. I was unable to stop in time to avoid the accident.

Incredibly, one's first instinct is to offer an excuse or to blame another.

In the Garden of Eden temptation (Genesis 3), Adam and Eve yielded to the temptation rather than maintaining the mandate of their Creator. When God confronted Adam about the disobedience that had taken place, what was the first utterance Adam offered to God? His excuse was, the woman you gave me caused me to disobey. Adam chose to blame God. When God confronted Eve, she had an entirely different response. She blamed God as well. Her rationale was, the serpent You created told me it would be alright. Eve chose to blame a created being. The responses of Adam and Eve continue on in the approach to human needs of people today.

It is especially true and has become too easy in the larger cities of this nation to become immune to the countless homeless people on the streets. It has also become too easy to avoid such people and to pass by and wonder what went wrong without reaching out to help. Why is it that we have become so calloused, curious and becoming far more interested in the details of what, why, when, and where, than we are about how we can help?

An example of this is introduced in John 9:1-2, "As Jesus went along, he saw a man blind from birth. His disciples asked him: Rabbi, who sinned, this man or his parents, that he was born blind?" The disciples' curiosity was about why he was suffering and that outweighed any desire to reach out to him. Were the disciples concerned about what they could do to help this man? Did they have any modicum of compassion for him? One of the followers of Jesus was a Medical Doctor. Would he pause and determine if there was anything that could be done to assist this man? It appears that lurking beneath the disciples' questions was a desire to know who to blame for the problem.

Within the Church, the list of excuses is never-ending. Missionaries and church ministries too often hear, "We can't afford to do this!" However, if there was an examination of the misguided priorities one has embraced and believe are excusable, much more kingdom work could be done and accomplished. Sports stadiums are occupied by some professing Christian people, who if they were asked to sacrifice the cost of a sporting event ticket for the cause of Christ would, in many cases, be met with mundane excuses. Forgotten in all of this is that God knows the heart and is keeping a detailed record. Oh? Obviously, change is needed! Will you put an end to your excuses and blaming of others? Prayerfully consider these things with me.

To Remember:

The Master is never pleased with one's
excuses and will never accept them as being valid.

67. Gifts and Giving

Perspective and Reality Moment

Have you ever paused to think about the values one embraces and how they apply to all areas of one's life? Not the least of these is the avoidance of personal debt, especially through the use of credit cards and the high interest rate that is assessed to the balance owed. All one needs to do is to go to the store of your choice, be it Wal-Mart, Best Buy, any big box stores and you will see people incurring debt at an exorbitant rate. These businesses know the propensity of people and have special sale days and hours as the enticement to spend that which one doesn't have for items that one cannot afford. Special Sale days start on the day after Thanksgiving. They name it appropriately, "Moonlight Madness or Black Friday." With all of the lecturing and counsel on fiscal responsibility given by conservative economists, such as Dave Ramsey, people ignore it all because they want their children, family and friends to be happy. They should heed the adage that suggests: "If your outgo exceeds your income, your upkeep will be your downfall."

When it comes to gifts received (or given), even the atheist would not quibble with whether the 25th of December is a winter holiday or a day commemorating the historic birth of Jesus Christ – yielding to calling it CHRIST-mas Day. The focus for an atheist is on a gift received or given, not on the day or what it is called. If we allow ourselves to get back to basics, we would ask: "If this is the birthday of Jesus Christ, why aren't we giving him presents and having a party for Him?"

Over the years, our family tried to remember the reason for the day. We did the routine of a birthday cake and the singing of happy birthday to Jesus. For the past several years, there is a greater awareness of special needs and ample opportunity of ministering to the needy, homeless, disenfranchised, orphans and the helpless in our communities, country and world:

- The Salvation Army collecting our monetary donations outside of a business.
- Angel Tree - a ministry of Prison Fellowship (and local churches) where gifts are received so they can be given to children and families of prisoners.
- Samaritan's Purse - the Shoe Box Ministry and giving practical supplies, as well as toys and games to children throughout the world.
- Jimmie Hale Mission in Birmingham, AL that economically feeds the homeless and hungry.
- Palmer Home for Children in Columbus, MS where children are housed, fed, provided a home setting with house parents, and assistance in their education.
- French Camp Academy in French Camp, MS where children are housed, fed and educated in a house parent setting.
- St. Jude's Hospital for children.
- Shriner's Hospital for children.
- Wounded Warriors and the care for military veterans who were wounded or injured in combat.

The list could easily be extended to include other worthwhile efforts and ministry. The above are among the more credible and most efficient in their use of funds and materials.

It is easy to become annoyed through mail solicitations for one to borrow money. Blank checks are sent so you can fill in for up to $5,000.00, or more, that will enable you to consolidate your bills and make that special purchase.

67. Gifts and Giving

WARNING - you will pay dearly for that borrowed money! I love the words of Proverbs 30:7-9,

> "O God, I beg two favors from you before I die. First, help me never to tell a lie. Second, give me neither poverty nor riches! Give me just enough to satisfy my needs. For if I grow rich, I may deny you and say, "Who is the Lord?" And if I am too poor, I may steal and thus insult God's holy name.

Let us retain our focus on The One, Jesus Christ, and His concerns for all kinds of people and their varying needs. At Christmas-time, one would do well to focus upon whose birthday is being remembered and celebrated.

To Remember:

I love the words of a Christmas Lyric that bring us back to a focus and commitment, especially at Christmas:

> What can I give him, poor as I am?
> If I were a shepherd, I'd give him a lamb.
> If I were a wise man, I would do my part.
> What can I give him? I'll give him my heart.

> (~ Christina Georgina Rossetti ~)
> (Public Domain)

In the Christmas Song about the Little Drummer Boy, in between the drum sounds are these lyrics:

> Come, they told me – A newborn King to see.
> Our finest gifts we bring – To lay before the King.
> So, to honor Him – When we come.

As one can glean from all of the lyric, the Little Drummer Boy identifies with being a poor boy too. The touching ending to the song is the drummer boy playing his drum for the newborn King. He honored the King with the best he had to offer.

68. Character Counts

Perspective and Reality Moment

Several years ago, a popular program on television was: "To Tell The Truth"! Three contestants attempted to confuse and stump a panel in terms of a position they held or an accomplishment they had achieved. Only one contestant was bound to tell the truth. After the panel had made their assessments and cast their vote, the host would say: "Will the real ____, please stand up!" We are well past the point where this should be the approach with political aspirants, as well as other people within our society. Integrity has been sacrificed on the altar of ambition and the position sought.

We don't often get to know who a person really is, nor do we get enough information to be enabled to discern what a person believes. A person can develop a narrative or resume that extols personal achievements. Some of the narrative may be exaggerated. The idea is to convince the interviewer that you can do the job or hold the position being considered. There was a Book Review of a tome entitled: Habitudes: Images that Form Leadership Habits and Attitudes by Tim Elmore. The reviewer shared this observation: "The iceberg is a great picture of leadership because so much of our influence comes from qualities we can't see on the outside. It's stuff below the surface. I estimate 90 percent of our leadership is made up from our character."

Candidates vacillate in their responses because they are trying to appeal to as many people as they can just so they can gain or win and hold an office. The principle of truth is clearly enunciated in Proverbs 12:17, "Whoever speaks the truth gives honest evidence, but a false witness utters deceit." And Proverbs 23:23 states, "Buy truth, and do not sell it; buy wisdom, instruction, and understanding." This is saying to us that we should value and cherish the truth. We should be unwilling to sacrifice or compromise the truth at any time or for any reason. There needs to be a way to challenge a person or candidate to stand up and To Tell The Truth.

Cynicism continues to increase when one hears a former President once again parsing words and engaged in re-writing history in order to project a position that is palatable to a greater cross-section of people. Why is he doing this? He is hoping to solidify a position and gain votes so perhaps his wife or his personal choice for office can win in a caucus or primary. The hope is that people will respond like sheep and be easily led. But - one should remember that being a sheep has inherent risks. Sheep are just as easily led to the slaughter as they are to the pasture.

Jesus Christ was making a spiritual appeal when he stated in John 8:32, "and you will know the truth, and the truth will set you free." That same truth has political and societal application. Truth should be cherished and promoted in discourse with people. Tim Elmore makes a very interesting comment in the aforementioned book. He states: "People are either thermometers or thermostats. They will merely reflect the climate around them, or they will set it. Leaders develop values and principles to live by and set the tone for others."

This is where we find ourselves today - desiring and searching for truth while being fed interpretations, nuances and parsing of details and facts to create a certain narrative, image and climate. We owe it to ourselves and the generations that follow to be champions of the truth, and only the truth. Never sacrifice or compromise it.

To Remember:

Since Jesus Christ is the Truth,
we should attempt to think His thoughts

68. Character Counts

and to speak His words.

69. Reformation Lifestyle

Perspective and Reality Moment

The reformation lifestyle for the biblical Christian and Church is concerned with how one is to fit into and function in a secular world. We can be aided by the biblical guidance in the high priestly prayer of Jesus Christ. In John 17:14-19, Jesus is praying about the distinctive lifestyle of His followers. He prays to the Heavenly Father about His own: "I have given them your word, and the world has hated them because they are not of the world, just as I am not of the world. I do not ask that you take them out of the world, but that you keep them from the evil one." This portion of His prayer allows there will be a tension between the secular world and the distinctive spiritual and reformation lifestyle. The prayer of Jesus continues: "They are not of the world, just as I am not of the world. Sanctify them in the truth; your word is truth. As you sent me into the world, so I have sent them into the world. And for their sake I consecrate myself, that they also may be sanctified in truth." The high standard for which Jesus prayed is that sanctification should be apparent as His followers die more and more to self and live more and more unto Him and His righteousness.

Another aspect of the reformation lifestyle is the knowledge and implementation of Romans 12:2 (ESV), "Do not be conformed to this world, but be transformed by the renewal of your mind, that by testing you may discern what is the will of God, what is good and acceptable and perfect." One's attention is again drawn to the tension between conform and transform. It implies that part of the tension is caused by the innate pull and desire toward pleasure and prosperity. This is magnified by the call for a disciplined commitment to a different lifestyle. The renewal of the mind where one will be able to think biblically and rationally. As the transformation process is developing, there will be a clearer definition and determination of God's good, acceptable and perfect will. For those who hesitate, rebel or are dissuaded by lesser things versus submission to the will and purpose of God, there is this word in Isaiah 46:8-10 (NIV),

> "Remember this, keep it in mind, take it to heart, you rebels. Remember the former things, those of long ago; I am God, and there is no other; I am God, and there is none like me. I make known the end from the beginning, from ancient times, what is still to come. I say: My purpose will stand, and I will do all that I please."

This is the God who requires transformation within His followers and expects compliance with His will and purpose.

This same emphasis on the reformation lifestyle can be seen in the reasoning of John as he writes, First John 2:7-8: "Beloved, I am writing you no new commandment, but an old commandment that you had from the beginning. The old commandment is the word that you have heard. At the same time, it is a new commandment that I am writing to you, which is true in him and in you, because the darkness is passing away and the true light is already shining." John is emphasizing that a transformation must occur because the laws of God are constant; the old commandment is foundational to the Word that is being heard; and the transformation is represented by the cloud of darkness that is passing away. It also emphasizes the true light that has pierced the darkness and is already shining. The question to consider is: What is that true light revealing and disclosing? John makes that known in First John 2:15-17,

"Do not love the world or the things in the world. If anyone loves the world, the love of the Father is not in him. For all that is in the world—the desires of the flesh and the desires of the eyes and pride of life is not from the Father but is from the world. And the world is passing away along with its desires, but whoever does the will of God abides forever."

The directive is clear and plain: Do not love the world; do not love the things that are in the world. A crucial and determinative factor and lifestyle choice is: "If anyone loves the world and the things that are in the world, the love of the Father is not in him."

John goes on to write why this is a threshold factor for the biblical Christian. He states that it is because all that is in the world (secular culture) such as the desire and lusts of the flesh; the desires and lust of the eyes; and the boastful pride of life is not from the Father but from the world. The foolishness or absurdity by the one ignoring God's Word is obvious. It is found in the focus and understanding of the biblical Christian in First John 2:17, "The world is passing away along with its desires, but whoever does the will of God abides forever." The struggle one may have in this area pertains to when the world will pass away. This is the designated and final moment for human history. Many are hoping that they have plenty of leeway for their desired lifestyle before any climax of the age. If this is their reasoning, they are making the same error as the people of Noah's day. They, like them, have convinced themselves and believe they have time to make the adjustments to that lifestyle before any climactic event occurs. It must be noted that anyone ignoring the clear truths declared by John is doing so to his own peril. There is no marginal reformation lifestyle. No one can straddle the fence between the two lifestyle choices. It is similar to the principle set forth by Jesus Christ in Matthew 6:24. "No one can serve two masters. Either you will hate the one and love the other, or you will be devoted to the one and despise the other." Jesus is speaking about one's attachment to money and things. The principle is clear for all issues in one's lifestyle choice. The tottering on the picket fence of decision will ultimately result in harm and disaster.

It is obvious that the visible church and professing Christian needs to return to the basics that are stated in Psalm 1:1-2 (ESV), "Blessed is the man who walks not in the counsel of the wicked, nor stands in the way of sinners, nor sits in the seat of scoffers; but his delight is in the law of the Lord, and on his law, he meditates day and night." The paraphrase in the NLT is, "Oh, the joys of those who do not follow the advice of the wicked, or stand around with sinners, or join in with mockers. But they delight in the law of the Lord, meditating on it day and night." The Psalmist is stating that which should be obvious for all from the outset. There is a certain innate allurement and progression toward evil. The dangers intimated focus on the shift of one's comfort zones regarding the prevailing evil of the world's culture and influences. The Psalmist states it in a mandate format:

- Do not walk in the counsel and advice of the wicked;
- do not allow yourself to stand in the chosen pathway of sinners; and
- do not become so enticed and comfortable with that which is contrary to biblical values that you allow yourself to actually sit in the company of those who scoff at true religion, the reality of God, the clarity of Scripture and the values contained within them.

Succumbing to these alternatives to biblical faith and practice gives evidence of the dangers of an undisciplined life. It manifests dangers and drift of one who is willing to make a place in his life for the enemy of the soul. At the same time, it is also making room for the source of evil to infiltrate one's life. The stain on one's soul is through one's allowing an opportunity for evil to infiltrate where godliness and righteousness are to exist exclusively. It is a demonstration of one's failing to know and heed the precise words of Ephesians 4:27, "give no opportunity to the devil."

A valid question for consideration is: "Why is care required by the biblical Christian in this area?" The answer is given in the text, Hebrews 10:38, "The just/righteous are to be living by faith." When permissiveness in lifestyle choices is allowed, the cultural trends and the societal emphases will result in negative influences to be encountered and engaged by the biblical Christian and church. It should be understood that cultural chaos and societal issues being promulgated are not conducive to the required Christian faith and practice.

The biblical Christian and church is to know only righteousness as a lifestyle and message that is embraced. An example of cultural chaos and societal preferences dominating the landscape is described in the days of Noah, Genesis 6 through 9. The population of that day did not want God or His Word as a viable part of their culture or society. The specific conditions that began to prevail are indicated in Genesis 6:5-9, "The Lord saw how great the wickedness of the human race had become on the earth, and that every inclination of the thoughts of the human heart was only evil all the time. The Lord regretted that he had made human beings on the earth, and his heart was deeply troubled. So, the Lord said, I will wipe from the face of the earth the human race I have created and with them the animals, the birds and the creatures that move along the ground for I regret that I have made them. But Noah found favor in the eyes of the Lord. This is the account of Noah and his family: Noah was a righteous man, blameless among the people of his time, and he walked faithfully with God." It is interesting to note that Peter describes Noah as: "A preacher of righteousness" (Second Peter 2:5). This description might come as a surprise. We know Noah built the ark that saved the remnant of humanity from divine judgment. In the process of building the ark, did he also preach to anyone who came to observe the construction of the ark? The people may have come to mock the effort of a man undertaking such a project. How did Noah respond to them? If he preached, what did his sermons sound like and what would they have conveyed?

The account of Noah in Genesis 6 through 9 does not include a record of any sermon that Noah preached. It does say that he was "a righteous man, blameless among the people of his time, and he walked faithfully with God" (Genesis 6:9). Noah's life was a testimony to the righteousness of God. If you were in a discussion group and had to guess what the sermon was that Noah would've preached, what would your response be? We may get a glimpse and insight from the words of Jesus in the Olivet Discourse, Matthew 24:37-44, "For as were the days of Noah, so will be the coming of the Son of Man. For as in those days before the flood they were eating and drinking, marrying and giving in marriage, until the day when Noah entered the ark, and they were unaware until the flood came and swept them all away, so will be the coming of the Son of Man. Prayerfully consider these things with me.

To Remember:

To live by faith and to be sanctified
by the Word leads to our gaining the
reformation lifestyle.

70. The Secret Place

Perspective and Reality Moment

A very compelling Poem was written by Ellen L. Goreh (1852-1937) and later set to music by George C. Stebbins (1846-1945). Miss Goreh was a high-caste native of India. After her conversion to Christianity, she spent a number of years in the home of an English clergyman, and wrote the poem. Once set to music, it at once came into general favor, and the deeply spiritual tone of the words brought blessing to many. Very soon it found its way into all parts of the world. Dr. Hudson Taylor, head of the China Inland Mission, stated at Northfield, Massachusetts that it was the favorite hymn of his missionaries. Some of the words are:

> In the secret of His Presence,
> how my soul delights to hide!
> Oh, how precious are the lessons,
> which I learn at Jesus' side!
> Earthly cares can never vex me,
> neither trials lay me low;
> For when Satan comes to tempt me,
> to the secret place I go.
> Would you like to know the sweetness,
> of the secret of the Lord?
> Go and hide beneath His shadow:
> this shall then be your reward;
> And whene'er you leave the silence,
> of that happy meeting place,
> You must mind and bear the image,
> of the Master in your face.

James Perry

Finding a secret place to meet and commune with the Lord is central in The Sermon on the Mount. Jesus instructed His followers about the things they needed to be guarded against, as well as the intimacy they could have with Him, Matthew 6:5-8 (BSB):

> "And when you pray, do not be like the hypocrites. For they love to pray standing in the synagogues and on the street corners to be seen by men. Truly I tell you, they already have their reward. But when you pray, go into your inner room, shut your door, and pray to your Father, who is unseen. And your Father, who sees what is done in secret, will reward you. And when you pray, do not babble on like pagans, for they think that by their many words they will be heard. Do not be like them, for your Father knows what you need before you ask Him."

The inner room, closet or quiet place is to make it possible for one to be completely focused on the business at hand, namely prayer, communion and fellowship with the Lord. In Matthew 6, this directive is then followed by the illustrative and model prayer of the Lord. If we personalize the prayer, it begins with, "My Father" indicating a personal relationship. It continues with words of worship: Your name be hallowed; Your kingdom come; Your will be done on earth. It is followed by personal requests: my need for His daily provision; my debts and trespasses to be forgiven by Him; and my need for deliverance from temptation and every evil way. This is all part of the learning process in the quiet and secret place with the Lord.

In terms of the secret place and being in the Lord's presence, an acquaintance from years ago wrote the following on January 1, 2015:

"I jotted down things God was pouring into my heart that first day of a new year because I felt that if I didn't jot them down I would forget a vision I felt like he was giving me for the year. Part of that was this: My prayer for this year is that I see him in all things and in all ways and trust that there is purpose and continue to know and truly believe that he is all I'll really ever need. In joy, in hope, in sorrow and in pain - I want to see and know more of my Jesus. In the fullest and best of days may my lips be full of his praise and in the dark and lonely days, my praise to him be even louder. May my trust in him grow ever deeper knowing I am exactly where I am supposed to be, that he is enough and will always be the only thing I really need and the only thing that will really ever satisfy me. The best is yet to come..."

I really and truly believe the Lord was reminding me, encouraging me, and commanding me to look for him in all things and in all circumstances because he promises us that we when we seek him with our whole heart, we will find him (Jeremiah 29:13). And he longs for us...for us to know him more and for us to know who we are in him. And when we look for him in all things, though we do not know what tomorrow will hold, we know we can face tomorrow because we know he holds the future, our time is in his hands and he is working out his plan for our lives...for our good and for his glory. It's often difficult in the world we live in and in the middle of our humanity to see how God can be in the midst of it all. But he is. I believe that with all of my heart. And knowing that he is in the midst of it all - that is so reassuring and can bring peace and comfort when we just can't quite understand.

Months after those words were jotted down our pastor presented what he would be preaching on for the next year...."Coram Deo" which is to live one's entire life in the presence of God, under the authority of God, to the glory of God. And, our theme verse for the year is Psalm 27:8, which says: You have said, 'Seek my face.' My heart says to you, 'your face Lord, do I seek.'

If we believe the Word of God to be true we must also believe that God is who he says he is. The two cannot exist independently. You cannot believe the word of God and doubt his character and you cannot believe God is who he says he is without believing His Word. If we believe he is who he says he is and his word is true, we can have confident assurance that he is in the midst of all things. And when we look for him in the middle of our circumstances (good or bad), he is faithful to his character. He does not change, he does not lie - he is who he says he is."

Each time I read this testimony and commitment, it thrills my heart and brings blessing and refreshment to my own soul. This young woman is a lovely and intelligent person. She has made a difficult but rewarding decision to live her life in the presence of God. I wonder why the number is not greater among today's young people who are willing to count all for loss so they may see and know Jesus Christ more fully and intimately. If only, we would identify with and believe the words penned by David as he communed with the Lord, Psalm 16:11 (NASB), "You will make known to me the path of life; In Your presence is fullness of joy; In Your right hand, there are pleasures forever." If we gloss over the words of Scripture, we do so at our own personal cost and deprive ourselves from the riches of knowing the Lord intimately. We also miss out on much of the abundant blessing that He longs for us to have and enjoy. The only way for one to know and receive is by coming before the Lord on His terms and not on our own. The refrain to a contemporary Christian song written by Steve Green is:

70. The Secret Place

Oh, I want to know You more!
Deep within my soul I want to know You,
Oh, I want to know You.
To feel Your heart and know Your mind…
Oh, I want to know You more.

To Remember:

Fullness of joy is a result of abiding in Christ
and His Word abiding in you.
Happiness changes with the circumstances
of life and is temporary at best.
Choose abiding in Christ and desire that
for all of your life – and then live your life accordingly.

Prayerfully – consider these things with me.

71. Confusion and Consternation

Perspective and Reality Moment

One of the heart-rending things to observe is when a person you have known very well over the years begins to slide into forgetfulness and the confusion that accompanies it. For them personally, there is a measure of consternation (the feeling of anxiety and dismay). My wife and I visited a widow in the local Nursing Home whose husband had been a long-time Pastor in another town. She would have moments when she would stop in mid-sentence and forget where she was –or – not be able to complete her thought. She tried to explain to me how her mind had become like a gear that had lost a tooth or two and would not mesh and work like it should. Since I had known her and her husband for a few years, I assured her that together we would piece together what she was trying to remember.

We have had frequent opportunities of visiting with one who had a very productive teaching career. She excelled so well that parents wanted their children to be taught by her. A personal concern she had was her ongoing inability to remember and recall. The concern was borne out of the fact that both of her parents had experienced dementia and the drift of one of them into Alzheimer's. She now finds herself in a similar plight. Despite her previous activities and energy level, she now finds herself uncertain and with an increasing amount of forgetfulness. Some people are willing to leave her alone during this time of drift. Others are willing to be patient and persevering as they try to converse with her in as normal a way as possible.

It is difficult to discern and accept when a person involved in the public eye begins to show these times of mental drift and fading. Another minister and I had done combined services from time to time. His wife was beginning to fail mentally and not able to fully express herself. She eventually, slowly, slipped into Alzheimer's. Following a service where we both had participated, when the two of us walked to where the congregation would be exiting, she came by and said to me: "I don't know where I'm supposed to go." I replied: "Just stand here between your husband and me and you will be fine." She managed to smile and seemed so relieved to know where she belonged and felt safe. The key is to relate to the person in as normal a way as possible for as long as one can.

A Scripture passage references how the Body of Christ should show a readiness to "accept one another." I see another application for those whose minds are failing, where they are drifting toward dementia and possible Alzheimer's. Romans 15:1-2, "We who are strong ought to bear with the shortcomings of the weak and not to please ourselves. Each of us should please his neighbor for his good, to build him up." This will involve a sensitivity toward those who often repeat themselves, as well as being unable to remember names, dates and places. It will also require patience as one slides through these various stages. Another verse that makes me think of a way through this wilderness journey is Psalm 22:19 (ERV), "But you, O Lord, do not be far off! O you my help, come quickly to my aid."

One of the encouraging acts that the biblical Church can do is to always include the person who is enduring the trial of memory loss. In actuality, it is more frustrating for them than it would be for you. If the person repeats something that had just been said, don't point it out or make a correction. This, too, is a frustration for the person. As an act of kindness, help the person through the rough places. Remind them of your name or where the next activity is taking place. A simple: "Let's walk together to our next meeting place or destination."

71. Confusion and Consternation

Some things that could be done in the past may not work as well in the present. Don't call on the person to lead in prayer or to quote some Bible verse or story they have shared previously. Be kind, considerate and helpful. It will mean a lot. If they happen to make a comment out of context, thank them for sharing what was on their heart at that moment and move on. Prayerfully – consider these things with me.

To Remember:

The Lord's Words in Isaiah 43:4-5 (NLT):
You are precious to me.
You are honored, and I love you.
Do not be afraid, for I am with you.

72. Coping with Loneliness

Perspective and Reality Moment

In general, when one is younger and with a growing family, life is anything but calm or lonely. There are always various activities and projects that need to be done. It is at such a time that one wistfully thinks about how nice the "empty nest" will be when quiet and order is once again restored to the household. It will be a time when parents can order their own lives and have their own conversations on an adult level that is free from incessant interruptions, needs that must be attended to and schedule maintenance. Charles R. Swindoll writes about this in a devotional titled: Someday. He wrote the following thoughts:

> We will return to normal conversations. You know, just plain American talk. 'Gross' won't punctuate every sentence seven times. 'Yuk!' will not be heard. 'Hurry up, I gotta go!' will not accompany the banging of fists on the bathroom door. 'It's my turn' won't call for a referee. And a magazine article will be read in full without interruption, then discussed at length without mom and dad having to hide in the attic to finish the conversation. Yes, someday when the kids are grown, things are going to be a lot different. One by one they'll leave our nest, and the place will begin to resemble order and maybe even a touch of elegance. The clink of china and silver will be heard on occasion. The crackling of the fireplace will echo through the hallway. The phone will be strangely silent. The house will be quiet... and calm... and always clean... and empty... and filled with memories... and lonely... and

we won't like that at all. And we'll spend our time not looking forward to Someday but looking back to Yesterday. And thinking: Maybe we can babysit the grandkids and get some life back in this place for a change!"

The heart and mind of God allowed in the creative order (Genesis 2:18 - NASB) that: "It is not good for the man to be alone; I will make him a helper suitable for him." The writer of Hebrews reminded those who are the body of Jesus Christ – His Church – about a starting place for benevolent care and personal interaction. Hebrews 13:1-3 (NASB),

> "Let love of the brethren continue. Do not neglect to show hospitality to strangers, for by this some have entertained angels without knowing it. Remember the prisoners, as though in prison with them, and those who are ill-treated, since you yourselves also are in the body."

A normal behavior is expected to be taking or making necessary time to show concern for or interest in another individual who may be alone or lonely. Showing hospitality to strangers will lift the loneliness of the empty nest and allow for personal interaction with new acquaintances. They may possibly become new friends.

It is good to recall that regardless of any human contact, the Lord has promised repeatedly that He always cares and is always with us. I appreciate the words in Psalm 27:10 (NLT), "Even if my father and mother abandon me, the Lord will hold me close." The rendering in the ESV is: "The Lord will take me in."

In 1920, Robert Harkness penned the words to a Hymn that should encourage the lonely person:

On life's pathway I am never lonely,
my Lord is with me, my Lord divine;
ever present guide, I trust Him only,
no longer lonely, for He is mine.
Refrain:
No longer lonely, no longer lonely,
for Jesus is the Friend of friends to me

Can you pause and look at the acquaintances you know and ask yourself: Do they need a friend? Are any of them trying to cope with personal loneliness? When did you last contact them to determine how they are and to see if there is an area where they need assistance.

There is a very powerful story that occurred with the approach of Hurricane Irma in September 2017. The report reads:

"Pam Brekke broke down in tears while waiting at Lowe's before Hurricane Irma hit when she saw Ramon Santiago receive the store's last generator. Her main concern was Richard Robinson, her 87-year-old father-in-law and Korean War veteran whose oxygen machine, which needs electricity, helps keep him alive at night. That's when Santiago, who doesn't speak English well, approached Brekke and asked her what was wrong. I told him: I'm just scared this storm's coming and my father-in-law is on oxygen. I'm just scared. And I said: That's all right, God will provide. And then I turned to walk away. Then he stopped me. And he said: Ma'am, this generator is for you. You take it. You need it more than I do. Most acts of kindness go unnoticed but this one was captured by a news team stationed at the store to capture people preparing for the storm and that which they deemed to be the most important item. The pair was able to meet again this week. And fortunately, under much better circumstances. Both weathered the storm safely. The two met up at an upholstery factory where Brekke works. The two exchanged a big hug. Santiago explained that just seeing Brekke in tears was enough to act and that giving up his generator was a no-brainer.

It is obvious that if or when an act of kindness is necessitated, it will entail a degree of personal inconvenience and a willingness to practice self-sacrifice. The man had a right to keep the generator even though it was the last one in the store. Some people might have done so. However, the biblical Christian does not have that option. The instruction that should be adhered to is Philippians 2:3-4 (BSB):

> "Do nothing out of selfish ambition or empty pride, but in humility consider others more important than yourselves. Each of you should look not only to your own interests, but also to the interests of others."

We readily admit that this is sometimes easier said than done. The *summum bonum* (the highest or chief good) which should be implemented in the biblical Christian's life appears in Philippians 2:5-8, "Let this mind be in you which was also in Christ Jesus: Who, existing in the form of God, did not consider equality with God something to cling to, but emptied Himself, taking the form of a servant, being made in human likeness. And being found in appearance as a man, He humbled Himself."

This is what we should emulate as we minister in Christ's name selflessly. Prayerfully – consider these things with me.

To Remember:

72. Coping with Loneliness

James 2:14-17 (BSB)

What good is it, my brothers, if someone claims to have faith, but has no deeds? Can such faith save him?

Suppose a brother or sister is without clothes and daily food.

If one of you tells him: Go in peace; stay warm and well fed, but does not provide for his physical needs, what good is that?

So too, faith by itself, if it is not complemented by action, is dead.

73. Seeing Jesus Only

Perspective and Reality Moment

When I first entered the vestibule of a former Hotel in 1954, the property was then owned by and operating as Columbia Bible College (now Columbia International University), one of the first things to gain my attention was an engraved marble inscription on a mantel that stated the purpose of the college and the desired goal for the students: "To Know Him and To Make Him Known." The school hymn would indicate the ways and means for this goal to be attained. Two of the stanzas emphasized:

All for Jesus, all for Jesus!
All my being's ransomed powers:
All my thoughts and words and doings,
All my days and all my hours.

Let my hands perform His bidding,
Let my feet run in His ways;
Let my eyes see Jesus only,
Let my lips speak forth His praise.
(Mary D. James – 1871).

When a Presbyterian Denomination began in 1956 (Bible Presbyterian Church, Columbus Synod), they also started Covenant College in St. Louis, MO. My wife and I realized, and appreciated, the incubator effect of Columbia Bible College. It was a great atmosphere for study and preparation for the Lord's work. The foundational bible courses and instruction has proven to be invaluable. But - what about this new college? Would it be a place where the same goals would be prominent and before the students? Would it be a place where the challenge to seek the will of God and His choices for one's life would be emphasized? Much to our delight, the theme verse of the institution was Colossians 1:18, "that in everything he might be preeminent." Additionally, the purpose hymn was also: "All For Jesus."

The schools had embraced the commitment of the Apostle Paul when he said (Philippians 3:10 ESV): "that I may know him and the power of his resurrection, and may share his sufferings, becoming like him in his death." He had on other occasions made known this same commitment, Romans 12:1-2 and Galatians 2:20 where his emphasis was on becoming a living sacrifice and being crucified with Christ. The emphasis was on where one must ultimately be with a personal commitment and then be able to meaningfully say:

> Not I, but Christ, be honored, loved, exalted;
> Not I, but Christ, be seen be known, be heard;
> Not I, but Christ, in every look and action,
> Not I, but Christ, in every thought and word.
> ~A.B. Simpson ~

Those who make a commitment to "All For Jesus" will soon realize there will be tests and challenges to ascertain whether or not such a commitment to the Lord is sincere or not. To serve as a measure of one's priorities regarding foundational principles, in First Corinthians 3:11-15 Paul reminds us of those things that matter most:

> "For no one can lay a foundation other than the one already laid, which is Jesus Christ. If anyone builds on this foundation using gold, silver, precious stones, wood, hay, or straw, his workmanship will be evident, because the Day will bring it to light. It will be revealed with fire, and the fire will prove the quality of

each man's work. If what he has built survives, he will receive a reward. If it is burned up, he will suffer loss. He himself will be saved, but only as one being snatched from the fire."

Peter writes in a similar way to the believers who will be facing a time of physical persecution and scattering and indicates, First Peter 1:5-7 (BSB), Who through faith are protected by God's power for the salvation that is ready to be revealed in the last time. In this you greatly rejoice, though now for a little while you may have had to suffer various trials, so that the authenticity of your faith—more precious than gold, which perishes even though refined by fire—may result in praise, glory, and honor at the revelation of Jesus Christ.

A key phrase is: "the authenticity of your faith." Is one endeavoring to live in the presence of God? Is one desiring the purpose and will of God for his/her life? In an Inauguration speech, John F. Kennedy made this comment to the world: "Let every nation know, whether it wishes us well or ill, that we shall pay any price, bear any burden, meet any hardship, support any friend, oppose any foe to assure the survival and the success of liberty."

With slight modification, should the follower of Jesus Christ be any less committed than: "We shall pay any price, bear any burden, meet any hardship"? This is the type of commitment Paul shared with the Philippian believers when he wrote, Philippians 1:20-21 (BSB),

I eagerly expect and hope that I will in no way be ashamed, but will have complete boldness, so that now as always Christ will be exalted in my body, whether by life or by death. For to me, to live is Christ, and to die is gain.

Such a commitment is challenging and demanding. While there may be a willingness and readiness to emulate this commitment, there will be many interruptions and interferences that can easily sidetrack one who wants his/her life lived all for Jesus.

This is part of the issue and discipline in choosing the narrow way. There is no promise that the pathway will always be smooth. The promise is that the Lord will always be with you whether the path is smooth or rough. One should never stray far from Isaiah 41:10 and Isaiah 43:1-5. The Lord's promise is sure. He means what He says – "I will strengthen you and help you." In other words, His grace will always be sufficient for you, me – us!

As we have continued to learn more of what it means to know Him and to make Him known, my wife and I have always found a great place of refuge and encouragement in the words of Isaiah 40:29-31 (ESV):

> He gives power to the faint, and to him who has no might he increases strength. Even youths shall faint and be weary, and young men shall fall exhausted; but they who wait for the Lord shall renew their strength; they shall mount up with wings like eagles; they shall run and not be weary; they shall walk and not faint.

To this day, our prayer continues to be:

> Teach us Thy way, O Lord, teach us Thy way.
> Thy guiding grace afford, teach us Thy way.
> Help us to walk aright – more by faith, less by sight,
> Lead us with heavenly light – teach us Thy way.

Prayerfully – consider these things with me.

To Remember: Isaiah 30:21 (NIV)

73. Seeing Jesus Only

"Whether you turn to the right or to the left,
your ears will hear a voice behind you, saying,
this is the way; walk in it."

The Lord's sheep always hear His voice and follow Him!

74. Thy Way

Perspective and Reality Moment

The obvious starting place is Genesis 1:26-30, the creation of man and his becoming a living soul. When he was created, man had been told by the creator that anything he would ever need would be bountifully provided. At this point, man also had full knowledge of God and His will; the reality of complete righteousness; and perfect holiness. Man had experienced unhampered fellowship with God on a daily basis – in the cool of the evening. That was - until - the serpent entered into that perfect place and infiltrated the thinking of both Adam and Eve. The serpent, being crafty and subtle, began by asking a question: Did God really say? For Eve, it stirred her level of curiosity, unguardedness and allowed her to talk with the serpent. These two realities – curiosity and unguardedness - can damage and hamper the most devout person. Just a momentary contemplation of the alternative can bring about great spiritual harm. Although the chief end of man is to glorify God and enjoy Him forever, Adam allowed for the beguiling alternative of increased and enhanced knowledge so he could become – literally – equal to the creator.

The distraction and the fall of man was immediate. He was driven from the Garden of Eden and began to experience the consequences of his disobedience. Romans 5:12-20 discloses that all mankind suffers because of the one man's sin. It also reveals the role that Jesus Christ fulfilled to redeem fallen man from his sin. Paul wrote: (V.12) "just as sin entered the world through one man, and death through sin, so also death was passed on to all men, because all sinned." He goes on to state the great transition that took place in Jesus Christ: (Vs. 18-19)

"Therefore, just as one trespass brought condemnation for all men, so also one act of righteousness brought justification and life for all men. For just as through the disobedience of the one man the many were made sinners, so also through the obedience of the one man the many will be made righteous."

This restoration process of man brings him back to the meaning and privilege of the image of God through and in Jesus Christ alone. When one comes to Jesus Christ for redemption, the process of man's return toward his pre-fallen estate begins. We learn from Colossians 3:10-14 that: "The new self is being renewed in knowledge in the image of its Creator." The new life changing process includes a renewed spiritual growth. It can be identified as the wardrobe of God's elect people: "Clothe yourselves with compassion, kindness, humility, gentleness, and patience. Bear with each other and forgive any complaint you may have against one another. Forgive as the Lord forgave you. And over all these virtues put on love, which is the bond of perfect unity." Man is transformed as he is "being renewed in knowledge."

Additionally, in Paul's instruction regarding the ramifications of knowing Christ, Ephesians 4:20-24 instructs: "You were taught to put off your former way of life, your old self, which is being corrupted by its deceitful desires; to be renewed in the spirit of your minds; and to put on the new self, created to be like God in true righteousness and holiness." The new self, "created to be like God" is the return to true righteousness and holiness.

This is in keeping with the words of Jesus Christ in Matthew 5:48, "Be perfect as your heavenly Father is perfect." And, First Peter 1:15-16, "But just as he who called you is holy, so be holy in all you do; for it is written: Be holy, because I am holy." This is how man was created to be and this is how God wants man, in Jesus Christ, to be.

Prayerfully – consider these things with me.

74. Thy Way

To Remember – Hebrews 12:14

No one will see God if he lacks true knowledge, true righteousness and true holiness.

75. Spiritual Awakening

Perspective and Reality Moment

Reference is often made to the plea and prayer of David in Psalm 85:5-7 (NASB) for spiritual revival: "Will You be angry with us forever? Will You prolong Your anger to all generations? Will You not revive us again, that Your people may rejoice in You? Show us Your lovingkindness, O Lord, and grant us Your salvation." David had a sense of the spiritual dearth (a scarcity or lack of something) that can so easily creep into one's life and Church, resulting in coldness to the things of God.

In this nation in the early 1700s, this malaise was sensed and had become the spiritual drift in the British-American colonies. Bursting on the scene were two dynamic men, Jonathan Edwards and George Whitfield. They were key to a spiritual revival that swept throughout the colonies. Jonathan Edwards, the Yale minister who refused to convert to the Church of England, became concerned that New Englanders were becoming far too concerned with worldly matters. It seemed to him that people found the pursuit of wealth to be more important than John Calvin's religious principles. Edwards forcefully declared: "God was an angry judge, and humans were sinners!" It was reported that he spoke with such fury and conviction that people flocked to listen. It became known as The Great Awakening. Out of that time of forceful declaration of God's Word came his sermon: "Sinners in the Hands of an Angry God." Many people were brought to tears and came repenting of their sins against a Holy God. Even apart from the preaching, people were brought to conviction along the roadside and in their homes. Many tears of repentance were being shed.

In addition to Jonathan Edwards (1703-1758), George Whitefield (1714-1770) was a minister from Great Britain who toured the American colonies. An actor by training and with good stage presence, he would forcefully declare the word of God, weep with sorrow, and tremble with passion as he delivered his sermons. Colonists flocked by the thousands to hear him speak. He converted slaves and a few native Americans. It was reported that the religious skeptic Benjamin Franklin had come to hear him speak in Philadelphia and was also impacted by what he heard. What was so unique about the ministry and sermons of Jonathan Edwards and George Whitefield?

In part, it was a dramatic shift and break from the Church of England and the formalism, rituals and traditions it represented. Additionally, there was an emphasis on the centrality of prayer. A servant of the Lord who is committed to church revitalization has shared: "Prayer is the most critical and essential element in the DNA of a local church. Martin Luther said: Prayer is the daily business of the Christian. John Calvin said: We see that nothing is set before us as an object of expectation from the Lord which we are not enjoined to ask of Him in prayer. John Wesley said: There is nothing without prayer." At a unique time in 1850, Jeremy Lamphier had been hired as a lay missionary by the Dutch Reformed Church in lower Manhattan to spearhead a visitation program to bring back a steadily declining membership. His efforts, for the most part were unfruitful. Parishioners were listless and unresponsive to his visits and the decline in attendance continued. He made a decision to start a prayer meeting at the noon hour that would be focused on spiritual awakening. The Fulton Street Prayer Meeting began in 1857. At the first meeting, just six men gathered in the rented hall on Fulton Street in New York City. America in 1857, was in crisis. The political climate was directionless. The nation was pre-occupied with discussion about slavery. The southern states were contemplating leaving the union. The possibility of a civil war was the conversation of the day. Fear, doubt and uncertainty filled the hearts of people in both the Northern and Southern States. For many, living conditions had become difficult to the point of being unbearable. The poor and poverty were glaringly present. Banks were failing. Transportation (railroads) were fearful of economic collapse. The Church that should've been the source of strength and spiritual awareness had declined and returned to liberalism, rituals and empty traditions. It had lost its vision and vitality. As societal conditions worsened, the six men who had gathered to pray soon became a group with thousands calling upon the name of the Lord. One year later, by May of 1858, secular newspapers reported, there were fifty thousand new converts to Christianity in New York alone. One paper reported that the New England area had been so profoundly impacted that in some towns, there could not be found one adult who did not profess Christ as their Savior.

Do you believe prayer is vital and powerful for your life? Do you believe prayer is vital and powerful for the revitalization of the local church? Do you believe that an answer to prayer for revitalization may include people from every tribe, tongue, nation and people? Do you believe that if faithful and godly people came together for prayer with a hunger in their hearts for the presence of God to be their reality, they would realize His answer in a dynamic manner? Where do you believe you/we should focus on and what should we implement?

To Remember:

If we earnestly seek the Lord,
 He will hear us and be found by us.
(Jeremiah 29:12)

76. Desperate for Awakening

Perspective and Reality Moment

In a moment of uncertainty, confusion and fear, the Psalmist penned these words, Psalm 44:23-26 (NIV),

> "Awake, Lord! Why do you sleep? Rouse yourself! Do not reject us forever. Why do you hide your face and forget our misery and oppression? We are brought down to the dust; our bodies cling to the ground. Rise up and help us; rescue us because of your unfailing love."

Do you ever have those moments when you can identify with the words of this Psalmist? You find yourself in a desperate and near-hopeless situation and wonder – where is God when I so urgently need Him? You believe you have done everything that is right and proper before the Lord, but yet you feel rejected, forgotten and left alone in the midst of your personal fears and apprehensions? You think God is sleeping and ignoring you? You have allowed yourself to think of God in human terms rather than in supernatural realities?

One of the primary errors is in thinking that God would ever be asleep and ignorant of an individual's plight. The reminder is firmly stated in Psalm 121:4-8 (ESV),

> "Behold, he who keeps Israel will neither slumber nor sleep. The Lord is your keeper; the Lord is your shade on your right hand. The sun shall not strike you by day, nor the moon by night. The Lord will keep you from all evil; he will keep your life. The Lord will keep your

going out and your coming in from this time forth and forevermore."

What causes one to be living in Psalm 44 rather than in Psalm 121? Have you ever found yourself approaching Psalm 44 rather than resting securely in Psalm 121? At such a moment, is it possible that the Lord's perspective and purpose for one's life has been ignored or forgotten?

Dr. Harry Reeder has summarized the desperate need for awakening in his book, Embers To A Flame. His thoughts about revitalization concerns are:

> "The Scripture presents a paradigm of moving from spiritual decline and functional malaise to Spirit-engendered vitality. When the Lord directed his comments to the Church at Ephesus (Revelation 2), God's instructions to that church serve as a curriculum outline for Church Revitalization. Remember therefore from where you have fallen, and repent and do the deeds you did at first (Revelation 2:5). That is the three-fold paradigm: Remember. Repent. Recover (return to) the first things. Church revitalization or renewal is nothing more than following God's prescription for church health. It is a process by which we work at reformation, lead for revitalization and pray for revival. Church revitalization is the sovereign work of God's Spirit whereby He restores His people to spiritual and functional vitality that inevitably leads to statistical growth in conversions and Scriptural discipleship for His own glory and our own good."

During my first years of ministry, a friend gave me a book, Come, O Breath by James A. Stewart. The subtitle is, Awakening Messages. In his opening chapter, the Scotsman Evangelist states:

"The vast majority of Christians are living a sub-normal Christian life. The New Testament characteristics of power invincible, joy unspeakable, glory immeasurable and peace incomprehensible are strangely lacking in their lives. The Christian experience of the Church is not deep, intense or vital enough to meet her own needs, let alone the needs of the world. We are so sickly and feeble that we are not able to discharge the functions for which we exist. We have adopted a policy of self-pity. The result is that we have the invalid's groan instead of the warrior's shout. We are absolutely powerless before the appalling conditions of the world today. The Church cannot give what she does not possess. It is the Church that is unbelieving, apathetic and worldly."

Where does awakening need to begin? With God? He neither slumbers nor sleeps! With you? Ephesians 5:14 states who will benefit from and who are among those whom the light must awaken! Could it be that malaise (a feeling of discomfort or uneasiness) has inflicted those who are called God's people? Are we more oriented to the status quo than we are to God's revitalization? In Revelation 2:1-7, when the Lord is described as walking among the Churches, what is the primary area He points out about the Church at Ephesus? The threefold paradigm is given to "Remember, Repent, and Recover (return to first things)." A primary focus the Lord shares with the Church is stated in Revelation 2:4, "But I have this against you: You have abandoned your first love." Those words need to be internalized by all of God's people today: "You have abandoned your first love." Is it possible that God's people no longer crave the intimacy, passion and presence of the Lord Jesus Christ in one's personal life? The very thought of it should penetrate deep within one's soul: "I no longer love the Lord as I once did!" Even if this is marginally correct, it should drive one to his/her knees before the Lord. The determination should be to remain there until the correction that is sought becomes one's reality. Is this something you need to do – should do - now?

One concern of the revivalist preachers in the early 1700s was the state of worldliness that had been embraced by the people. Materialism had become the primary focus rather than biblical adherence. There are many ways to describe the culture and church in America in the twenty-first century. Materialism and worldliness stand out among a longer list of departures from spiritual truth and commitments. That which seems to have become distorted and misrepresented defines how great the drift has become in terms of worldliness. It seems as though the key words in First John 2:15-17 have been blotted out of the memory of many people today, and sadly, that includes professing Christians as well. What did John write and what did he mean? Remember the words he wrote:

> "Do not love the world or anything in the world. If anyone loves the world, the love of the Father is not in him. For all that is in the world—the desires of the flesh, the desires of the eyes, and the pride of life—is not from the Father but from the world. The world is passing away along with its desires, but whoever does the will of God remains forever."

The direct statement that should arouse concern among the professing Christians is: "If anyone loves the world, the love of the Father is not in him." Does that remind you of what the Lord stated to the Church at Ephesus in Revelation 2:4, "You have abandoned your first love"? Jesus was very clear in what

He stated and meant in the sermon on the mount, Matthew 6:19-21,

> "Do not store up for yourselves treasures on earth, where moth and rust destroy, and where thieves break in and steal. But store up for yourselves treasures in heaven, where moth and rust do not destroy, and where thieves do not break in and steal. For where your treasure is, there your heart will be also."

In other words, Jesus wants us to focus on the eternal and not the temporal. Where is your focus? What are your values? How would Jesus Christ assess them?

If our thoughts and actions were subjected to magnification and three-dimensional projection, how horrible would they appear? How ashamed would we be? Would there be a sense of guilt and neglect in any projected area? If so, what should we do about it? Would any personal action take place in the immediate or would there be an inordinate delay? Do we believe that God knows our deeds and words? Within the Church you attend, even if a revival series has been announced and planned, has there also been an anticipation that God would bring about conviction and repentance among any of the congregants? If He did, do you believe it would impact you? Your church? Your community? Prayerfully – consider these things with me.

To Remember:

One must be exposed to The Light
if any spiritual break-through is to occur.
If we were conduits for The Light,
we would know more about who God is,
what God does as well as what He will do.

77. Leadership Awakening

Perspective and Reality Moment

Spiritual awakening and church revitalization do not just happen apart from careful thought, preparation, effort and prayer. It requires godly people hungering for the presence of God and an outpouring of His Spirit. It is a desire for new life and vitality. It entails a vision of God's desires and an obedience to His directives. To achieve this goal, there should be - there needs to be - a core of faithful men/witnesses (Second Timothy 2:2): "The things that you have heard me say among many witnesses, entrust these to faithful men who will be qualified to teach others as well."

Could it be that we are living in a day when the culture has so infiltrated the church that godliness is no longer the norm nor the desire of men's hearts? Can this occur in the twenty-first century Church? Is it occurring and steadily increasing among professing Christians? The commentary about the church is similar to the words of Micah 7:2, "The godly person has perished from the land, and there is no upright person among men."

One of the very practical contributors about the need for awakening and that which may hinder it is offered by James Emory White. He began a Church Plant 25 years ago and has been Senior Pastor of the work from the beginning. In reflecting on those 25 years, he has written a soon to be published book – *What They Didn't Teach You In Seminary*. A portion of that book includes: "25 Years Of Leadership Lessons." Just a few of his lessons are:

- Fads and styles, models and trendsetters, will come and go. Stay focused on one thing: the mission.

- You'll grow bigger and faster if you focus on transfer growth. Don't. Reaching the unchurched is what it's all about.
- On any and every issue, go to the Bible and then go with the Bible.
- Prize character over talent, and loyalty over just about anything.
- Resolve to prioritize children's ministry. Once again, you'll find it to be the Best. Decision. Ever.
- The key question to ask isn't how to grow the church; the key question to ask is what is keeping the church from growing.
- You don't possess every spiritual gift. Don't operate as if you do or let others expect it of you.
- Your competition isn't, and never will be, another church. You're after the person who doesn't give a rip about churches.
- Your core values are the hills you should die on.
- Left to itself, the natural flow of the church is to turn inward, grow older and become outdated. Leadership must intentionally combat all three.

Too many churches that are dwindling continue to fall into the trap of looking inward resulting in their becoming maintenance type efforts. Caring for the older members is great but ministry must never be limited to doing just that. There is also a need to consider and evaluate the leaders of the particular congregation. Are they godly men of vision and prayer? A goal for leadership is summarized in Acts 6:4, "Brothers and sisters, choose seven men from among you who are known to be full of the Spirit and wisdom. We will turn this responsibility over to them." Was this a good decision? Would there be a good result from this action?

There are a series of summary verses in the Book of Acts that characterize the result of a praying church and a qualified leadership. Can ordinary men accomplish the extraordinary in the name of Christ? A first summary answer given is in Acts 6:6-7 (ESV), "The apostles prayed and laid their hands on them. And the word of God continued to increase, and the number of the disciples multiplied greatly in Jerusalem, and a great many of the priests became obedient to the faith."

A second summary verse is Acts 9:31 (BSB), "Then the church throughout Judea, Galilee, and Samaria experienced a time of peace. It grew in strength and numbers, living in the fear of the Lord and the encouragement of the Holy Spirit." A transition that occurred in this section is the conversion of Saul of Tarsus. He soon became a dynamic and daring witness for Jesus Christ.

A third summary is Acts 12:23-24, "Herod, who opposed the Gospel and refused to give glory to God, was slain when an angel of the Lord struck him down...But the word of God continued to spread and multiply. Despite Herod's intransigence (unwilling or refusing to change), in the midst of that challenge and adversity, God honored His Word, the Holy Spirit moved among the people, and rather that eradication there was multiplication.

A fourth summary is Acts 16:4-5, "As they went from town to town, they delivered the decisions handed down by the apostles and elders in Jerusalem for the people to obey. So, the churches were strengthened in the faith and grew daily in numbers." The key words in this summary are "strengthened" and "grew" daily in numbers.

What do you think? Can this happen in your local church, community, area? Has it ever been prayerfully considered? Is there a readiness to make changes? When was the last time these criteria was central for the spiritual leadership in your church? Recently? Ever? Prayerfully – consider these things with me.

To Remember:

Church revitalization can only occur
when it is done God's way and by God's means.

78. If I Could I Would

Perspective and Reality Moment

Most men, after completing their scholastic requirements for ministry, eagerly anticipate where they will go to serve the Lord. They have an excitement and enthusiasm as they venture into their new place of ministry for the Lord. They also have an expectation that the church or ministry that has issued them a call has a similar excitement, enthusiasm and expectation. Deep inside of the young servant is a series of goals along with the idea (perhaps ideal) of if I could I would do the following. The initial issue is that an existing congregation, albeit it subtly, has allowed itself to leave the innovative behind as they have drifted into being set in their ways. Two older and mature Pastors shared with some of us younger ministers that it is great to enter ministry with our ideals intact. They suggested that they be placed in a hip pocket and never be forgotten. They continued to state an obvious truism that most churches don't share those ideals and that which is best.

The usual focus of church boards and congregations is on a philosophy of ministry. It amounts to what a minister and the church leadership embrace as the functional priorities. It would be excellent if the priorities were always Scriptural. If both could or would embrace a passage such as, Ephesians 1:5-12 (ESV) that states the main foundational principle (especially in verse 6): "To the praise of his glorious grace, with which he has blessed us in the Beloved" and verse 12, "We who were the first to hope in Christ might be to the praise of his glory." That fits nicely with the answer to: What is the chief end of man? The response is: "Man's chief end is to glorify God and enjoy Him forever." Other aspects of the

Philosophy of Ministry include: Exalting the Lord in all ways and all things (First Corinthians 10:31 and Colossians 3:17); Equipping the saints to do works of ministry (Ephesians 4:11-16); and, Evangelizing the lost (Acts 1:8, Matthew 28:19-20). Why are these things so frequently omitted?

Another area where there also needs to be focus and purposeful interest is in the Psychology of Ministry. In a cursory research of the subject (Bible.org), one point that is made and seems constant is: "What are we supposed to do when the problems of daily life seem insurmountable and no one seems to care enough to listen or suggest solutions?" A study from a decade ago suggested that hundreds of ministers abandon ministry each year due to moral failure, spiritual burnout or contention within their local congregations. If this is reality, does it matter to the average congregant or church association? In a day of political and societal pressure, Peter wrote to the Church – First Peter 4:7, "The end of all things is near. Therefore, be alert and of sober (sound) mind so that you may pray." Paul wrote to Timothy similar words, Second Timothy 1:7 (NKJV), "For God has not given us the spirit of fear; but of power, and of love, and of a sound mind."

We need to think about the pastor and the pew. The idea about having a sound mind and being self-disciplined is important. When I do not have the privilege of ministering God's Word as a Pulpit Supply, my wife and I make it a point to visit one of the smaller congregations. At one time, these churches were viable and maintained a reasonable attendance. While sitting in the pew to worship, it is often obvious that the one conducting the service is disappointed that the attendance is so limited and small. The question above surely comes to mind when a handful of people are desirous of preserving their church and so few seem to care enough to faithfully attend it. Legitimate excuses aside, when a minister stands in the pulpit to declare God's truth and so many don't seem to demonstrate care, it can be very disappointing, discouraging, and in some cases – depressing. He can even allow himself to think - if the membership doesn't care, why should I? It is a time like this that the one who arrived at the congregation with eager expectation realizes that the - if I could I would - hope has vanished. The ideal has been crumpled and the minister's eagerness to serve effectively has been dashed.

If a Church is to be revitalized, there needs to be a gathering of those whose commitment is at the very least, the expression of Psalm 122:1, "I was glad when they said unto me, let us go into the house of the Lord." And the words of Psalm 97:12, "Rejoice in the Lord, you righteous; and give thanks at the remembrance of his holiness." There is an increasing need for firmly committed biblical Christians who will be loyal to the Savior Who has called them out of darkness into His glorious light (First Peter 2:9-10). Prayerfully – consider these things with me.

To Remember:

Psalm 37:5 reminds us to commit our way to the Lord.
Proverbs 16:3 reminds us to commit our work to the Lord.
If we do, we will succeed. If we don't, we will fail.

79. To Be Like Jesus

Perspective and Reality Moment

The Apostle Paul shared his heart when he wrote to the Philippian believers about his personal priority (Philippians 3:10-11), "I want to know Christ and the power of his resurrection and the fellowship of sharing in his sufferings, becoming like him in his death, and so, somehow, to attain to the resurrection from the dead." His goal and purpose was to be like Jesus and to become more and more like Him each new day. Even though he had a sense of his human qualifications in the competitive secular world, he considered that as being the category of rubbish so that he might know His Lord more completely

He shared his religious credentials (Philippians 3:4-6), "If anyone else thinks he has grounds for confidence in the flesh, I have more: circumcised on the eighth day, of the people of Israel, of the tribe of Benjamin; a Hebrew of Hebrews; as to the law, a Pharisee; as to zeal, persecuting the church; as to righteousness under the law, faultless." These two statements by Paul demonstrate the tension that exists when one's pursuit in life is for personal achievement or recognition (See: Chapter 62, Name-Droppers). Whether they deserve it or not, some people receive recognition and acclaim due to either their persona or crafted resume. They tend to eagerly bask in the acceptance and acclaim of their peers. Meanwhile, others who have considerable merit and ability fail to receive recognition or acceptance as being one who qualifies for some measure of human honor and respect.

A recent devotional asks a series of questions and submits answers about one's focus and personal sense of self-worth. They include:

Are you trying to discover your self-worth? You have it in Him—He died for you!

Are you plagued by failure and guilt? He does what no one else will or can do for you—He forgives and forgets, kills the fattened calf as heaven rejoices (Luke 15:22-24), and clothes you with the best robes of His righteousness.

Are you searching for significance? Search no more—you are His child. There is no greater significance than that.

Are you trying to figure out your life and wondering if there is any purpose for you on this earth? The mystery is unraveled in Him as He leads you to live for His glory and to reflect the reality of His character."

There is a simple and basic Worship Chorus about personal commitment that should be remembered by each servant of the Lord:

To be like Jesus, to be like Jesus;
All I ask - to be like Him.
All through life's journey,
From earth to glory,
All I ask - to be like Him.

Paul has a simple resolve regarding the best choice one can make when confronting this tension. It is stated in Philippians 3:7-9,

"But whatever was an asset to me, I count as loss for the sake of Christ. More than that, I count all things as loss compared to the surpassing excellence of knowing Christ Jesus my Lord, for whom I have lost all things. I consider them rubbish, that I may gain Christ and be found in Him, not having my own righteousness from the Law, but that which is through faith in Christ, the righteousness from God on the basis of faith."

If you aim high, you will find true worth, value and acceptance in Jesus Christ. If you aim low, you will find frustration, anxiety and lack of sensing any acceptance or at all.

A dear lady in the first church where we were privileged to serve the Lord had a difficult marriage and personal physical issues. She was advanced in years but faithfully would rise early and sit on her front porch with her Bible on her lap. As she opened it, she would pray: "Lord, you have given me another day to live for you. You have promised in your word that as your days, so shall your strength be (Deuteronomy 33:25). I need your strength for this day. Thank you. Amen."

Charles Haddon Spurgeon shared the following thoughts on Deuteronomy 33:25: "How often do we find out our weakness when God answers our prayers! I asked the Lord that I might grow In faith and love and every grace, might more of His salvation know and seek more earnestly His face. I hoped that in some favored hour at once He'd answer my request, and by His love's constraining power, subdue my sins, and give me rest. Instead of this He made me feel the hidden evils of my heart and let the angry power of hell assault my soul in every part! Lord, why is this? I trembling cried:

> Will You pursue Your worm to death?
> 'Tis in this way,' the Lord replied,
> 'I answer prayer for grace and faith.'

That is, the Lord helps us to grow downward when we are only thinking about growing upward! Let any of you try to grow in grace and seek to run the heavenly race - and make a little progress - and you will soon find in such a slippery road as that which we have to travel, that it is very hard to go one step forward, though remarkably easy to go a great many steps backward!"

As we pursue our journey along the narrow way, that same strength from the Lord is available for you and me. Be encouraged as you make this journey along the narrow way. Prayerfully – Consider these things with me.

To Remember:

Walking with Jesus and living like Him requires one
to be humble, along with a readiness
to endure rejection, as our Savior did.

80. Shake Up - Wake Up

Perspective and Reality Moment

The News Headlines and Reports of August 2014 included some of the following: San Francisco Bay Area Assessing Damage After the Large Quake. The San Francisco Bay Area's strongest earthquake in 25 years struck the heart of California's wine country early Sunday morning, igniting gas-fed fires, damaging some of the region's famed wineries and historic buildings, and sending dozens of people to hospitals. The magnitude-6.1 quake, centered near the city of Napa, an oasis of Victorian-era buildings nestled in the vineyard-studded hills of northern California, ruptured water mains and gas lines, hampering firefighters' efforts to extinguish the blazes that broke out after the temblor (earthquake) struck at 3:20 a.m. The temblor (earthquake) lasted 10 to 20 seconds, according to the United States Geological Survey.

At first blush, this news report could be written about similar devastation in October 2017. Another headline - Lima, Peru - A large 6.9-magnitude earthquake has struck a sparsely populated area of central Peru, the U.S. Geological Survey said Sunday. Authorities were still surveying the region, including the Ayacucho area where the quake was centered. According to the survey's updated figures, the quake occurred at 7:21 p.m. EDT Sunday and was centered about 27 miles east-northeast of an area called Tambo, and about 290 miles southeast of the capital of Lima. It had a depth of 62.8 miles, the survey said. Local media said that the quake was felt in parts of Lima and in many major cities of southeastern Peru, including Cuzco and Arequipa.

The third news story stated a magnitude 6.4 earthquake shook the region near the Chilean port city of Valparaiso on

Saturday evening. The center of the quake, which was also felt in the capital city of Santiago, was 37 kilometers north of Valparaiso at a depth of approximately 40 kilometers, according to the seismological institute at the University of Chile.

Meanwhile, a fourth news story showed the gruesome video of an American Photo-Journalist being beheaded by a representative of ISIS (Islamic State in Syria). Also, at least 19 people have been beheaded in Saudi Arabia during August 2014 in a clampdown by the authorities on drug smuggling and sorcery, according to Human Rights Watch officials. Four hashish smugglers were beheaded - the latest in a string of executions across the country since the beginning of the month, Saudi Press Agency reported. All four were men from the same family, reported the Independent, while another suspect, Mohammed bin Bakr al-Alawi, was beheaded for practicing black magic sorcery.

Just some extraneous thoughts: What if God was employing these means to gain the attention of people in this nation and worldwide who have been ignoring Him? What if God was using these means to indicate that it is much later than one thinks in terms of God's eternal plan and purpose? What if God was allowing that the theological explanations, hermeneutical (interpretation of Biblical texts) and applications of man do not agree with His time schedule for His world? What if God was indicating that Luke 21:10-11 (along with: Mark 13:8, Matthew 24:7) is His now? Jesus said: "Nation will rise against nation, and kingdom against kingdom. There will be great earthquakes, and in various places famines and pestilences. And there will be terrors and great signs from heaven." What if God was saying to a world that is rejecting His Son that they need to give attention to Colossians 1:16-17, "For by him (Jesus) all things were created, in heaven and on earth, visible and invisible, whether thrones or dominions or rulers or authorities, all things were created through him and for him. And he (Jesus) is before all things, and in him all things hold together." What if God was indicating that if Jesus just slightly lessens His grip on this universe all kinds of cosmic-disturbances will occur? This could well be the last shake up – wake-up-moment and call to a culture slipping more and more into darkness.

What if God's bottom-line for us is He wants us to give attention to Ephesians 5:14-17, "Awake, O sleeper, and arise from the dead, and Christ will shine on you. Look carefully then how you walk, not as unwise but as wise, making the best use of the time, because the days are evil. Do not be foolish, but understand what the will of the Lord is." It's time to pay attention; assess the reproach that has been brought to Christ's Name and to amend one's ways. What if our nation, much like the City of Nineveh, responded affirmatively to the Lord and His Word? The "what if" possibilities should not be viewed as either irrelevant or frivolous. Christian commitment and church ministry should always operate on the cutting edge of that which is transpiring in the world. It gives opportunity for relevant input into the lives of people who may be devastated by raging fires, severe hurricanes and massive flooding. The loss of life through an act of terror gives opportunity to comfort those who are grieving. It is a moment when sharing food with the hungry, water with the thirsty, clothing to those who lost theirs in the floods or fires. The landscape of the times is the challenge to act in Jesus' name to meet the physical and spiritual needs of countless numbers of people. Prayerfully - Consider these things with me!

To Remember:

God's now is according to His plan, His timing and His determination alone. We need to be fitting our lives into His plan for them.

ACKNOWLEDGEMENTS

In one way or another, all of us are indebted to others for the contribution they have made in our lives. One's background is a contributing factor as well. My Mother became a widow when I was seven years of age. It meant that she would have to find employment to support her family. One of the early influences in my life was my maternal Grandmother. She was a kind soul and knew the Scriptures well. She would often couch what she said with some Biblical reference. Upon learning of her death, some of the local merchants made that similar statement about her quoting Scripture.

One person who had a significant influence in my life was a third-grade teacher who had become an Assistant Principal at the Public School I attended. She saw something in me that caused her to be a positive influence. I often wished that I could've made contact with her in later years to let her know that her investment of time and care in me had not been wasted.

In my preparation for ministry, a man who never finished High School worked for the city's sanitation department. He would not let the young people fall through the cracks and reached out to them, and especially with me. He would make certain that I had a good reason if I missed Church. His interest continued until his sudden death.

Another man who loved to walk each day around town would often stop by my office to see if I had time to pray with him. When he prayed, one had the sense that he was personally speaking to God who was present with him/us in the room.

Other later acquaintances have encouraged that I elongate some of the Blogs I've posted into this book format.

They are more recent and cherished friends. You will find them mentioned earlier in the book. If any benefit is gained by reading the book, gratitude is owed to several people alluded to and mentioned who helped to shape my life. I am indebted to them for their effort and time.

May the Lord bless and enrich you with similar friends and acquaintances who will have a similar positive influence in your life. My personal desire is that their tribe would increase. Their contribution for one's journey along the narrow way will model valid discipleship and lead others to follow Jesus Christ. To Him alone be all the glory.

About the Author

James Perry has served the Church with more than 54 years of continuous ministry. He attended Columbia Bible College (now Columbia International University) for three years; transferring to Covenant College, a new Presbyterian College in St. Louis, MO from which he graduated with a B.A. in Philosophy. After graduation, he enrolled in Covenant Theological Seminary where he received a B.D. in theology, and returned later for his M.A. He and his wife make their home in Centreville, AL; He has four children; 16 Grandchildren and 14 Great Grandchildren. He is the Author of 10 Books (all of which are available on Amazon).

Realizing Significance, 236 pages, The author summarizes the heart of this book. He explains: "We know about their existence (little people) and some of their needs but we can be so focused on "us", "me", or "I" that we miss seeing or caring for "them", "they" or the "unknown".

Taking A Serious God Seriously, 224 pages, is a clarion call for Christians to return to the standards of Scripture, because God is serious about how Christians should think and live in this world. Every chapter defines what it means to have a serious relationship with a serious God.

The Twenty First Century Church: Is It Waxing Or Waning, 226 pages, This book examines the contemporary church to see if it measures up to the standards of the Bible. It reveals the failure of the church in relationship to the biblical model.

Practical Awareness of Living in the Presence of God, 186 pages, The author wrote this book to give Christians a greater awareness of the Glory of the Lord's Presence in their daily walk and relationship with Him.

Amid the Cultural Chaos: Are We Casualties or Conquerors? 241 pages, Each chapter in this book throws out the gauntlet for Christians to choose a godly culture.

Trending Toward Cultural Captivity: Learning to Survive the Inevitable, 158 pages, This book examines some of the trends that have become overwhelming and a strong influence upon the direction of the nation and world.

Navigating the Cultural Maze: Searching for the Only Way Out, 147 pages, This book will provide you with challenging insights and encouragement to be a light shining into and piercing the darkness in your life.

The Right Course and the Only Right Choice, 154 pages, This book will help Christians gain greater insight in terms of their spiritual journey.